MW00626996

Welcome to our conversation.

Have any questions or comments regarding ideas in this book? Write to:

ira@theundercoverroad.com

Go to my website (theundercoverroad.com) to sign up for my free monthly newsletter and read all previous issues collected on the Articles page. Here is where I supplement the book with additional suggestions for making money, improving relationships, achieving success and pivoting to new careers. My goal in all these writings is to help you feel hopeful and prepared for a better life.

You will also find links on the website to my three social media pages that I post on regularly.

I have started a mentorship program to offer personal one-on-one guidance. Interested? Send me an email.

FOREWORD

THE UNDERCOVER ROAD is an insightful and unusual guide to creating the various components of a successful, balanced life: money, health, relationships, career, happiness, and personal satisfaction.

It begins with the premise that the culture, media, government, corporations and even educational institutions dispense fraudulent, misleading or unrealistic suggestions for achieving most people's goals in a Western, developed country.

After years of dead ends, frustration and unimpressive progress, the author, Ira Shapiro, discovered strategies and mental tools that turned his life around phenomenally. He succeeded to such a striking degree that he kept his approach hidden and under cover.

Now, Ira is revealing the attitudes, methods and observations that will unquestionably—with practice—bring readers closer to their individual life goals. This is a practical, frank offering replete with anecdotes about successes by other everyday people as well.

In down-to-earth chapters about less obvious ways to make big money and the details of reinventing yourself or starting up new businesses, the author also calls upon coincidence, intuition, and Asian thought. You will learn how your brain tricks you to avoid stress and discomfort in making major decisions involving your partner or your career. Ira shows you how to learn more about your likes and dislikes by examining the groups you have joined. You will discover the surprising benefits in traumatic setbacks. If you are out of step with most people, you will read how to exploit thinking out of the box to help reach your goals. If your views are more conventional, there are techniques to spur creativity.

Finally, there are chapters on determining your goals, spotting trends, changing your attitude and extremely practical tips about life that will enhance your enthusiasm, zest for each day and perhaps joy to be alive.

TABLE of CONTENTS

After you finish reading the Introduction, you can delve into the other chapters in any order that appeals to you.

NO NEED TO READ CHAPTERS IN SEQUENCE.

INTRODUCTION

THE UNDERCOVER ROAD

We are raised with fraudulent promises. Our culture, schools, the media constantly fool us with false routes to happiness and money. We are inadequately informed about health and diet. We are rarely told to seek wisdom. We are misled about love. We are lied to by politicians and corporations.

At 78-years-old, I feel obliged to share some secrets—secrets that will motivate and inspire you. I will emphasize making money, which buys survival, security, and a better chance at happiness. I will tell you how to pivot from where you are, no matter your age or career stage. I will suggest ways to reinvent yourself, a process I have done six times, so far. But you must be willing to take some chances, because doing nothing will result in stagnation or possibly have change forced on you like downsizing or obsolescence—that is something you don't want.

In my early thirties, I hit a dead end. I was full of failures and frustrations. Like most people, I had not reached my objectives. I wasn't even on my way: middling income ($26,000), unimpressive job, marriage ending, no prospects.

But by accident after a funeral, I was nudged onto a new path that made everything I wanted relatively easy to achieve. My life changed in a remarkable way. I didn't find a magic wand. I had to work at it and discover how to apply the principles I am going to teach you. In fact my successes were so phenomenal that I was embarrassed. The changes reached such a striking degree that I kept my methods hidden and under cover.

For decades, I have felt I was on the other side of a raging river, yet I crossed it. I looked back at all the people who were in the same place where I had been, who were struggling, and I knew that I needed to share how to cross that obstacle.

I am going to describe how I made millions of dollars, straightened out my life, and achieved my goals involving: careers, money, health, relationships, happiness, and personal satisfaction. It's an unconventional approach, takes effort to master, and is not for people who are afraid to deviate from the norm. My approach has not only worked well with regards to money, but it also works well in all aspects of life.

If your life is like mine was in my early thirties, you are struggling with obstacles, are confused about what direction to take, been thwarted and met failures despite doing what you thought was right, then you have nothing to lose by hearing what I will say. Give it a shot.

There is no doubt that I had many lucky breaks. But despite any hurdles you might face or burdens you are carrying with you, I am convinced that your chances of success will improve if you do what I learned from my experiences and those of pioneers before me.

Since I crossed that imaginary river, I have made many blunders. I have screwed up so badly that, at times, I have astonished myself. *How could I know so much, do so well, and still not call upon past experience to avoid giant mistakes?* We screw up because we all have our limitations, our blind spots, our periods of denying the realities in front of us. On balance though, I am sure that I have bumped into an unusual and successful approach for living an upper middle class or better life in a developed country.

You often read and hear about famous and successful people who are held up as inspirations and role models: Bill Gates, Steve Jobs, Albert Einstein, sports and movie stars, etc. These celebrities are exceptional, and copying their achievements is probably impossible. Their stories and journeys are definitely not yours or mine. If you could walk in their footsteps, you would already be on your way to fame and riches. Even if you are only in your teens or 20s. You wouldn't be frustrated enough to have picked up this book. You would have found the golden path long ago.

I didn't start on my road until I was 35. I was a late bloomer who was stymied for years by disappointment and fears of failure. Before that, I expended considerable effort trying to earn more money, but I could never "figure it out." I was terrified that I would be middle class all my life, constantly worrying about paying bills and providing a better life for my family.

I have since learned that sprinkled throughout the United States are huge numbers of people who have become millionaires. One report says that 10.1 million households have over $1 million, and that doesn't include the value of their home. That is one out of every 13 (or 7.5%) of all U.S. households. Another report says there are 13,500,000 millionaires, totaling 4% of the entire population or 5.5% of the adults. Can you believe there are so many?

You rarely read about most of them, because they are not considered newsworthy by the media. Nevertheless, many exist privately, quietly and well below the radar. They are often hidden and camouflaged. Quite a few rich people live frugally and without show and big-boy toys.

I have been a millionaire for three decades and want to paint a methodology and philosophy that has worked for me in all areas that are part of a full and fulfilling life. Not just money-making. The relative ease with which I can make most of my decisions and choices is what leads partly to such sweeping success. I think just being able to select one action over another is a very big deal. The next challenge is to pick the right option. I will help you learn how.

I am certain that most other millionaires and happy people have achieved their results in different ways than I have. It's not a contest about whose ways are better. Whatever works. But most important is that my words give you a realistic, unbelievably pragmatic strategy and outlook for your own future. I promise you that if you practice my suggestions, you will be amazed how simple some of the difficult choices will become.

For example, my biggest financial success so far was (in 1993, at age 52) co-founding with a 21-year-old a company now called Take Two Interactive Software Inc. It is a publicly owned company best known for the Grand Theft Auto franchise (GTA), whose latest edition had the biggest launch in history of any video game, movie, or any other entertainment product: $1 billion in sales in three days. GTA5 has so far sold over 130 million copies and generated sales over $6 billion, much more than the highest-grossing films of all time.

My friends, business advisors and professionals, even family members, all told me that I was nuts to take this risk. "Games are for kids," they'd say. There is no future in the field. Some knew that the father of my partner had spent time in prison for tax issues, and that was reason enough to not move forward. With eyes wide open, my wife and I invested in the business. It felt so right I couldn't stop myself. Back then we were the only funders willing to take that chance with our young partner. As time went on people with hundreds of millions of dollars invested into the field. Even though we sold almost all our shares by 2003, I am proud that in 2018 the company was valued above $15 billion, and video games are almost a $135 billion a year industry.

Take Two started as a CD-ROM company making travel discs, before most people had ever heard of a CD-ROM, and drives were not readily available. Even then, my young partner saw the future of games. I helped secure a team of game developers, long before they were plentiful.

Before Take Two, after being fired twice from salaried jobs, I co-founded, with just $800, a visual book publishing company that I owned solely for 20 of 27 years until the internet killed it. My wife and I also started a real estate renovation and land preservation business. The 2008 housing bubble-bursting put that in a deep sleep, so I began my fifth career as an angel investor again with my wife helping entrepreneurs start their businesses, sometimes based only on a PowerPoint or an idea written on an envelope. I am writing a book in the hopes that I can help you learn how to accept and grow from change. Perhaps, I found a sixth career?

I know not everyone can-or wants to-change careers, particularly if you went to school for years to become a doctor, lawyer, artist or worked in one industry or factory for decades. But being adaptable to market changes, new styles or societal needs is important if you want to make money, especially when you have only your labor to offer and haven't yet saved funds for investment. Rolling with, and dodging, life's frequent setbacks and difficulties is also the best way to overcome the hard times that have nothing to do with financial wellbeing.

YOU MUST BE FLEXIBLE. In college, I knew a physics major who admitted he no longer liked physics. He was a junior and had decided not to change his major because he already 'invested' two-years in this field. He made the choice to continue to pursue it for the rest of his life although he didn't like what he was doing. How crazy is that? Life is too short to be miserable when you have so many opportunities to be happy, or at least happier.

My intention is to describe a different point of view and an accessible philosophy that you will not learn from teachers or other books. You will need faith, belief, intuition, insights, hunches, and synchronicity. However, it is not a flighty, New Age method. Utilizing logic and your previous practical experience are essential. It simply uses parts of your brain's potential that are often overlooked in our sequential, rational, word-oriented society. Get ready to use your common sense!

I will also spell out some simple principles and basic strategies that I have acquired over the years, so that you don't have to re-invent the wheel and discover them on your own. These are lessons of life that have been useful for centuries, but never taught in school or by most parents. Why not take some shortcuts to your achievements? You can always try them out and discard the ones that don't work for you.

If you are a teenager, just considering what paths to choose, these ideas should be unbelievably useful. Those of you in your 20s and 30s already have many personal experiences to compare with what I am describing. You can look back and imagine how you might have applied my suggestions to your previous circumstances. You still have plenty of time to make major changes in how you make decisions and take action.

The older you are, the less likely you are to change and adjust your problem-solving, decision-making patterns. But even if you are over 40, I urge you to try to still move forward. As you will see, it is never too late to reach your goals.

Here are some of the subjects I will discuss in the following sections:

DISCOVERING GOALS, so you know where to go, and developing habits that will help you get there. It is a huge challenge. You have to know your strong and weak points to succeed. And the more specifically you can visualize your next set of goals, the better your odds of reaching that target.

EASIER WAYS TO MAKE MONEY than are taught in school and discussed with friends. Here is an area in which we are duped by bosses and society. There are so many ways to acquire money that you haven't thought of, so you'll find them spelled out. Many of these options will surprise you.

PIVOTING OR REINVENTING YOURSELF is scary but could be necessary. Where do you find the courage to make changes that might fail or lead to rejection? Millions of people have done it and are still doing it. Some aspects of this effort are obvious and basic. But maybe you haven't thought of them. You can do this at any age, whether to make more money, begin a new career, or succeed at enjoying better health, deeper relationships, more wisdom.

NEVER GIVING UP is easy to say, but very hard to do, especially if you have failed already. You will find useful suggestions here to motivate you to keep plugging and training yourself to not become disheartened.

JOINING GROUPS is what we do without thinking, whether for business, pleasure, religious support or to help others.

There are many benefits and confrontations in doing this. You will need to learn to compromise to be accepted and to get along. Most people don't realize how much you can learn about yourself through this process and interaction. It's a surprising opportunity to help determine your next directions.

EARNING THE RESPECT OF OTHERS is far more important than most people realize. Sometimes this need leads to life and death decisions. The more you appreciate how motivated you are by the opinions of others, the easier it will be for you to make ideal choices on your road to success.

CHECKING YOUR ATTITUDE is another challenge for you to examine. Changing your perspective to be more positive will alter everything you see and do in life. It will bring you more money, friends, peace and possibly joy. There are some techniques I have identified that will probably affect your outlook.

DISCIPLINE is essential, and I will describe easy ways to acquire it. Having plans that are never implemented will prevent you from reaching your goals. Execution is everything. You must give your dreams a chance to come alive, no matter how terrified you are of failing.

BEING DIFFERENT AND THINKING UNCONVENTIONALLY increases your odds at succeeding in many endeavors. If you have long felt out of step with your friends or peers, there are ways to take advantage of those distinctions. They can be blessings in disguise.

WHAT TO DO IF YOU AREN'T CREATIVE OR A VISIONARY and can't think any way but normally and conventionally. Learn techniques to boost you out of your ruts and grooves. You must take little steps to prime your creative pump. Some educators believe we are all creative and fearless as children but that schooling and social mores beat it out of us. There are ways here to bring those sleeping talents to life again.

SPOTTING TRENDS is crucial if you are considering making major life changes and career moves. You want to enter growing industries, like information technology, healthcare/eldercare and private spaceflight, rather than dying fields, like coal mining or newspapers. There are social changes like the gig economy, fake news, fleeing refugees or gay rights that you must be aware of. Environmental changes like rising oceans and increased pollution that will impact your possibilities. And technological innovations that are affecting us enormously all the time. Being aware of what some of these trends are can help you decide which road to take in your search for more income and a better life.

DEALING WITH TRAUMA is not always a bad thing, particularly if you are prepared for it. It's going to happen, but it can be incredibly beneficial. I will surprise you with how and why. But to go through your years without anticipating the hardships that you and those close to you are sure to encounter is naïve. It is always better to be prepared.

START-UPS are not for everyone, although 20% of millionaires who earned their own money did it by beginning or owning their own business. If you don't take that route, you can use some of your savings to back another person's dream. I will spell out how it works and describe my own experiences in this risky area with huge potential rewards.

COINCIDENCE, INTUITION AND HUNCHES are with you all the time—if you don't tune them out. They can be the source of your success in any pursuit. Everyone has them, but most people ignore them, because they don't make sense. These are vastly more important than you can ever imagine. They will assist you through the morass of decision-making that confronts you every day. Sometimes you will be so sure of what to do, even when it defies all logic, that you will fear you're going nuts. You're not. I will guide you to this place of unorthodox benefit.

FINDING AND NURTURING RELATIONSHIPS with a lover, your child, neighbor and associates. Understanding people and what they want is a great talent. There are thousands of books and classes spewing advice about how to do it better. I will distill what I have encountered to help you succeed in this area. No promises of perfect marriages, fame and crowds of admirers. But some less obvious insights that are sure to make interaction more enjoyable and positive. And I promise that suggestions here will be beneficial in business as well.

MAINTAINING GOOD HEALTH is more important than people imagine, until you lose it. Most folks have no idea how to be fit, lose weight, avoid illness. There is a limited benefit in being alive if you are sick or tired often. And you can't do your job well or advance your career ideally if you are distracted with health issues that could have been avoided. I think nothing is more important than health. Top of the priority list. Amazing that so many ignore it, until it is too late.

USING ASIAN PHILOSOPHIES AND MARTIAL ARTS STRATEGIES in your daily life to make you happier and better able to cope with the struggles of being alive. These are more useful in business than you could imagine. I built a successful publishing company using verbal aikido, when dealing with customers. They never had a chance, nor realized what was happening. Yet it was a win-win for all of us. You can learn much here, even if you never study martial arts or visit Asia and especially Japan.

PRACTICAL WISDOM and how to integrate it. No theoretical philosophy here, but savvy stories describing how to manage the real world. Good for acquiring money and reaching your other goals as well.

These tools and strategies above will be discussed and can be applied to everyday living and decision making: when you are shopping for clothes, cooking dinner, meeting with friends, making phone calls, wooing a lover. They can also help make you rich or affluent; or help you change how to earn a living and with a different group of people you enjoy being with.

I am no genius, no great brain, no intellectual. However, I am reflective and think all the time about my goals, past actions, future possibilities. I react to my situation, I can change, and most importantly, I never give up and neither should you.

CHAPTER ONE

DISCOVERING GOALS IS DIFFICULT

I used to write speeches and help handle the financial public relations for a very controversial tycoon. Early in his rise to notoriety, he bought a software design company and concluded that: The biggest obstacle to solving a problem was: identifying the right problem. Corporations spend millions of dollars on R&D when they aren't even sure what they are trying to solve; as do individuals, bureaucrats and small business owners. Before you start on a journey, you need to know where you want to go.

However, it takes more than just knowing the problem you want to solve and how to solve it to become a tycoon–it takes sacrifice. I remember being in his limo, when his wife was due to have a baby. "She had the baby this morning," he told us "...but I was at the birth of the previous kids, so I don't need to be there for this one. Let's focus on the business."

I was stunned. Was that what it took to acquire hundreds of millions of dollars? Maybe. I knew right then, that was not how I was going to measure my success. To me there needed to be a balance of money and happiness to be successful. To me, life didn't have to be like that, although I never made hundreds of millions.

Identifying the exact goal comes into play if you are trying to save money. People can save more easily if they have a specific item or use for the money to be spent on, like a house, car, or trip to Amsterdam. Saving for a 'rainy day' is much harder. However, maybe you can incentivize yourself by creating a pot of funds for your first investment, whether it be stocks, mutual funds or to back a start-up. I am convinced, by the way, that you need to have funds to invest to make any advances toward affluence or wealth.

It's too hard for the average person to reach that goal through money from labor alone. More on this later.

What is it that you want? Ask yourself. Do you go for what you want? One night at the end of a first date, I said good night to a young woman after a drink in her apartment. I went down the elevator to the lobby. Then I realized I had left my umbrella upstairs. I had read enough books about psychology and behavior to realize that it was no accident. Even so, I went back up, knocked on her door, sheepishly said hello and retrieved my umbrella.

After saying goodnight for the second time, I went back to the elevator quite confused. I squatted down against the wall and spent the next 20 minutes at least attempting to identify what I wanted to do. Stay with her or leave? I had been so respectful so far. I had played it cool. Not too forward. This was in the late 70s, and women's liberation had not yet taken over.

This was a very difficult effort. I kept talking to myself, attempting to not 'figure it out' or imagine what I should or shouldn't do. I had to ignore anything to do with her reactions or preferences. No concern about embarrassment or rejections. What did I want?

Eventually I connected, knocked on her door, and with great precision, told her what I wanted: "I would like to spend the night with you." I hadn't put the decision on her shoulders by saying, "Could I...?" or "Would you like to...?"

She was already in her nightgown, looking quite lovely. She smiled and said, "Come in..."

That evening was a major turning point for me. I risked being a fool, but I took a first, baby step in discovering what I want, what the problem or the end result really was, and accepting whatever happened. It was important to be clear about what I felt and what the goal was. In this case, there was a happy ending, for we saw each other many months.

Most importantly, I realized how hard it was for me, and maybe you, to uncover what I wanted—not just in spending a night with a first date. I had to practice diligently to identify my true desires. It took a long time, but became easier and quicker over the next few years. I'll tell you in a later chapter how you can do it, too.

One way is to notice what you don't like to do, especially when society and others near you are telling you how great something is or should be and how enjoyable it is or it is supposed to be.

I met a woman once who loved dinner parties that had polite, predictable conversation. Nothing controversial. Exactly the kind of evening that I found tedious and avoided. Dorothy said she felt very comfortable at those tables: she knew what to say, what others would say, didn't have to think about what to say, and wouldn't be put on the spot. Plus, she was able to dress up and be with her friends. Not for me...BORING!

Of course, there are gatherings around food that are pleasurable beyond the tastes for your tongue. Obviously, conversation can be stimulating, provocative and educational. You might like that kind of interaction. You may not be afraid of confrontational questions that put you on the spot and force you to respond publicly and quickly without reflective thought. If that is you, then you can accept it and move on. There is no right way. The goal is to find out who you are AT THIS POINT IN TIME, so that you can figure out what you want to do: what path in life you want to follow, where you might want to live, what kind of career you want, how much money you want, what kind of life partner appeals to you. These things will change over time and with experience, but at least get started along your road.

The one thing I knew in high school was that I didn't want to end up like so many of my father's deceased friends and acquaintances. He would read the weekly paper and frequently bump into obituaries of guys who passed in their 40s. Many were overweight and died of heart attacks. Too many pastrami sandwiches, cheesecakes and hard liquor. None of them exercised. They would sit and drink and play poker and gin rummy many nights a week.

I also knew that I didn't want to worry about money, but that I wasn't going to earn it by following my culture's tendency to become doctors, lawyers, accountants and retail merchants. None of those paths appealed to me. I was highly motivated to move on and out. I just didn't know where I was going.

I remember a 30-year-old co-worker in New York being stunned that I didn't yearn for a house in the suburbs with a white picket fence and rose bushes. She thought everyone wanted that life. I was just as flabbergasted that she could imagine such a set path was the preferred choice of everyone.

A few years later, when I lived in the suburbs, wore a three-piece suit, carried my round-cornered attaché case and commuted daily by rail to work in Manhattan, I saw body parts on the track from a man who may have jumped in front of the train. I didn't want to become that man, even in a spiritual sense. Someone who hated his life so much that the fate of the oncoming train seemed more promising.

But as a close and well-meaning friend said, it was time I gave up thinking about the dreams of a 17-year-old and to recognize what adult life was all about: You are a middle-income business man, a commuter, a father, a husband, and you should make money the best way you can. Accept your reality and stop thinking that your life will be different.

But I still couldn't accept that obvious path.

Do you know the story of the pied piper? A town infested with rats hires a man in pied (large irregular blotches of color) clothing to play his magical musical pipe (perforated wind instrument) and lure the rats with a tune into the river to drown. He does a brilliant job. But when the mayor reneges and refuses to pay for the service, the rat catcher seeks revenge, returns and lures all the children away, either to drown or disappear in a cave.

I see contemporary society through a similar lens: the culture, the media and our traditional values are luring us all down a path of conformity, restriction, indebtedness to the banks and credit card companies, and dissatisfaction. So many people are lonely and unhappy. Not everyone, of course. But so many feel they haven't enough money, even if they make hundreds of thousands or millions. Some try to keep up with their neighbors' expectations. Others spend hours improving their houses, buying the latest-styled clothes/cars/TV's, and going to parties to be seen.

They seem so confused and frustrated. They followed all the advice, all the rules, did what they were told, went to the right school or ate at the 'best' restaurants, bought the correct tie or the elegant earrings, or wore the hipster's black. Yet something, maybe many things, are clearly missing.

I have met those people often. They are not enthusiastic, or full of amazement, or uplifted, optimistic, radiant. Their lives are dull and depressing. They drink excessively, take tranquilizers and drugs. They are overweight, pallid, frequently sick or thwarted. They don't understand where they went wrong. They thought they were doing what they were taught and told to do.

On the other hand, I am on a hill, and it appears to me that the crowds are being seduced by a cultural pied piper who is leading them over a cliff. The masses are following naively, happily for the moment to be dancing and singing to the tunes of the group. They are glad to belong. They do not protest or ask if the path is a safe one or even one they like. Sometimes they have doubts, but they continue the journey towards a terrible end.

Why in the world would I take that road, when I can hear them screaming as they fall into the abyss. I just had to have the courage to take a different path. To go off on my own with less fellowship. I clearly was not like them, so it was never a choice. I just had to pull together a list of what I did like, and what worked specifically for me.

CHAPTER TWO

PIVOT OR REINVENT YOURSELF

Dream it, plan it, do it! Dream it, plan it, do it! Carve those words onto the road of your life, in the tunnels you travel through during your dark times, in the clouds when you are soaring freely with success.

There are two main reasons people choose to make serious career (and other) changes. You were finally brave enough to run from a job or situation that you can't stand anymore. You hate picking vegetables, working in an office, dealing with the public. Or you are drawn towards a career that you fell in love with, like a child seeing her first ballet, or you're excited to spend each day outdoors or around computers or with animals. The more you like what you do, the better you'll be at doing it.

Regardless of what motivates you, don't procrastinate. Pivot from the unhappy or dead-end situations. Reinvent yourself to add zest and enthusiasm in your life. If you do delay in making a life change, like so many of us (including me, of course), do it somehow, eventually, before it is too late, and your time to decide is over.

I spoke to Ann Middlebrook about how she reinvented herself, when she was in her mid-50s. She graduated in 1977 with an undergraduate degree in Speech Pathology. But never followed that path. I met her in the graphic books area, when she worked many years for my company, American Showcase. In fact, she was running it when I sold in 2004.

After that she became an independent consultant to various visual book publishers. When her mother died in 2008, Ann reevaluated her life. "I wanted to do something more meaningful. Making money for publishing clients no longer seemed of value."

Ann Middlebrook with Grandkids.

"One day I was having a conversation about this with my sister, and she said, 'Why don't you try to get a speech job?'"

"I thought she was crazy, because I had no experience in that field, but I decided to give it a try. I sent out applications and received several responses. At the time, there was a real shortage of speech therapists, so my certification was of value."

"The woman that interviewed me and eventually hired me kept asking me how I would do this and how I would do that. My response was always, 'I'll figure it out. I know I can do this.'"

Ann's business background was helpful. She felt that this was her calling. She was very sure of herself. To make a long story short, she was hired and did figure it out. She also had to go back to graduate school to upgrade to the current master's requirements.

Ann was driven. She was determined. So while teaching in public schools, she spent 4 1/2 years going to graduate school one night a week and then doing homework at night and on weekends. After five years at her first job, when her position was eliminated due to cutbacks, she found another position for a year. When she was RIFed (Reduction in

Force) again, she then found a third.

This one was her dream job. You can bet she is very proud—and rightly so—of how she changed her life, now that she is providing therapy for kids with disabilities, such as autism and ADHD. To her it is very satisfying to make such a difference.

Ann was fortunate enough to have a degree that she could use decades later, at a time when there was a shortage of people with her training. What if you don't have that education in another field? What if you don't have a sister who reminds you that you have a certificate from 32-years earlier?

Two movies come to mind with the answers: *McFarland USA* and *Stand and Deliver*. I love these films, both based on true stories. You should see them. Both are about disadvantaged kids who have no hopes or dreams for the future. A devoted teacher in each creates seemingly impossible challenges that result in students discovering they can be good at something. That breakthrough leads to confidence and college and total reinventions.

If they can do it–with all their obstacles, disadvantages, lack of role models and opportunities–then I am sure you can too. So, as you read their stories, think hard about anything that you are good at, any skill or interest that might set you apart from the average person and give you more confidence that you too can reach the next level in your life.

McFarland, California was 90% Mexican-Americans with kids picking crops since they were eight to 10 years old. And that is their future. After 16 years teaching science, wood-working, and Physical Education, Jim White, a Caucasian guy, starts coaching the boys and girls cross country teams. The students call him Blanco and they think the sport is for prep schools. But White convinces them to give it a try, makes them put in the effort to accomplish something, anything that will show them they can do more than be only field pickers.

These kids helped their families earn money by picking before and after school and on weekends. White accommodated their schedules, sometimes working in the fields with them to make up for lost time. He was totally committed. And they reciprocated. White and some of his runners had to convince skeptical parents who could see no value in the sport.

In 1987, McFarland's boys team ran first in the state. After that victory, the school won the state championship nine out of 14 years. Once other students saw what was possible, they rose to that formerly unimaginable level of excellence.

Every boy on the 1987 team completed college. Not one of their relatives before them had ever obtained a ninth-grade education. The Diaz family saw all seven kids run and go to college. Over the 23 years that White coached cross country, dozens of McFarland kids also completed college. That too was previously a ridiculous concept for those students.

I remember when Roger Bannister was the first man to run the four-minute mile in 1954. It had never been done. After Bannister, other runners started doing it. In fact, his record only lasted 46 days. The new record was broken three years later, but again that only lasted a year, and it continued like that 18 more times. The current record of 3:43:13 was set in 1999, and the sub-four-minute mile has been run at least

1300 times!

It's amazing what you can do if you see someone else or someone you know do it. It is a bigger challenge to accomplish a goal or a dream, when you are the first to take it on. Or if there is no mentor urging you.

The second movie, *Stand and Deliver*, is about Jaime Escalante, a high school math teacher in East Los Angeles in the 70s and 80s. He also fought the resistance of fellow teachers, his Hispanic students and their parents who could see no usefulness in math. The school was in danger of losing its accreditation, and Jaime was urged to teach at a low level to get by in disruptive classrooms.

He started teaching Advanced Placement (AP) Calculus. Unthinkable. The kids could barely do basic math, much less algebra or calculus. He promised them a future, college, jobs in engineering, electronics and computers, but they must learn math. And they had to have 'ganas,' Spanish for desire or motivation.

He teaches them on Saturdays and in seven-week summer sessions. He overcomes their low self-esteem. He fights skeptical parents and teachers who think he is shaming them and just plain naïve about what is at all possible.

When the first 18 kids passed the 1982 Educational Testing Service (ETS) national AP Calculus exam for college, ETS and school officials were certain the students had cheated. It was inconceivable that Hispanics from such low-income, problematic, working-class neighborhoods had the intelligence and ability to learn such a high-level subject.

Fourteen had to take it over, and 12 of them passed. The next year 33 took it, and 30 passed. By 1991, 570 of Jaime's kids had taken AP exams in math and other subjects. Many went on to college, their lives changed by their new sense of self. President Reagan visited Escalante after he became famous through the movie and a book about his extraordinary teaching accomplishments.

Jaime believed in his kids. He pushed them to excellence and their lives improved. But this is another inspiring tale of students with little hope and no great future whose mentalities–and then their lives–are totally changed by effort and belief.

You can do it too, can't you? If you try. Dream it, plan it, do it.

Ben Fernandez.

Here is yet another anecdote about a photographer I knew, Ben Fernandez. He came from Hispanic East Harlem, New York and worked as a crane operator in a shipyard in Hoboken, New Jersey, where he took pictures of his co-workers. Next, he worked at the Brooklyn Navy Yard, until it closed in 1963. He was 27 then and gambled on turning his photography hobby into a livelihood.

He got a job running the darkroom at Parsons School of Design. He would soon develop and build the photography department at the New School and later become Parsons' Photo Department chairman. All this in spite of being severely dyslexic and unable to read. Ben even earned his college degree at age 48 by having people read to him, and he answered essay questions by speaking out loud. What an achievement!

In the early 60s, he started the Photo Film Workshop in the basement of Joseph Papp's Public Theater in NYC. It taught photography to underprivileged kids, free of charge. Ben would raise grants and donations to support this passion. I remember being in that basement and seeing what he was doing. I recall him saying that some of the kids would hardly speak, had never handled a camera.

But under Ben's tutelage, they saw that they could do something they never imagined. They came out of their shells, they became confident in some of their abilities, and grew to believe they might have more potential than anyone could fathom.

Fung Lam graduated from Harvard cum laude and became an obstetrician. Llewellen Lennon became an architect, Leonard Morris became a successful commercial photographer with clients like Coca Cola and Angel Franco is a Pulitzer Prize winning photo journalist with *The New York Times*.

These four may be the Workshop's often-celebrated stars. But I am certain they represent the many reinvented lives of their buddies who came to believe in themselves after they learned they did not have to continue on the more limited path from their origins. Fifty years later, Ben's former students are still contacting him and emailing their thanks for how he changed their lives so dramatically.

You know it's a lot of work to move on to a new path. It takes a great deal of effort to figure out what you might be good at and what you might have passion for. You must identify what truly thrills you or at least makes you a tiny bit excited.

Then comes that gigantic effort of changing direction, sacrificing short-term pleasures and overcoming lazy inclinations to watch TV or play outdoors or spend more time with friends, enjoying conversation and good tastes and drinks.

You have to give some of that up to execute this reinvention thing that people refer to so casually. Even if you just pay attention and start noticing friends or acquaintances who are taking steps to become different. While writing these words, I am bumping into stories about strangers all the time now.

A woman wrestler I never heard of died at 46. She called herself Chyna Doll. She had a college degree in Spanish literature, was a trainee with the Peace Corps and thought of joining law enforcement. She eventually entered a wrestling school, even though she wasn't a fan of the sport.

"I'd been rejected at everything," she told *The Boston Herald* in 1999, describing unsatisfying efforts as a bartender, a saleswoman and a singer.

Watching a televised match, she said, she realized: "I could go out and be this big, huge female and entertain people. That'd be my niche."

That's a hell of a reinvention! Turns out she was good at it: She was the first and only woman to win the World Wrestling Federation's Intercontinental Championship in 1999, and won its Women's Championship in 2001. She went on to become a reality TV star. "It'd be a shame to waste my physique and desire. I think I can be the female Arnold Schwarzenegger," she told *The Houston Chronicle*.

The lesson here is to figure out what you have to offer. I

bumped into Chyna's obituary[1] in *The New York Times* (April 21, 2016). There are stories like these all around us, and if you are open to them, they will crowd into your life. Hopefully some will be inspirational and guide you to a different path.

I was telling some people about reinvention, when I heard about Bob Ross[2] for the first time. This celebrity was in the US Air Force for 20 years, rising to the rank of Master Sergeant. While in Alaska, he took an art class and discovered he was a natural. He took more classes, and then one year, while working part-time as a bartender, he saw a TV show called, *The Magic of Oil Painting*, which taught amateurs techniques for making a painting in half an hour. He later studied with the show's host, and realized he could earn more from selling his paintings than he was making in the military.

So Ross retired from the Air Force in 1981, and in 1983 launched his own PBS TV show, *The Joy of Painting*, which taught a quick-painting technique for 11 years in the US, and in Europe, Latin America, and Canada.

He went on to create an art supply business, wrote 20 how-to books, made 100 videotapes, and started a school that still teaches Bob's special techniques, with certified Bob Ross instructors who travel the world...a multi-million-dollar enterprise. He came a long way from yelling at airmen to clean their latrine. In fact, most viewers supposedly tuned in to hear Bob's soothing voice[3] and watch him paint, "happy clouds and happy trees." Very soothing in a troubled world. You can watch his videos on the Internet.

In an *Orlando Sentinel* interview, Bob gave some advice that sounds familiar: "I don't intimidate anyone. Instead, I try to get people to believe in themselves. I tell people, 'You can do this.' And they write back and say, 'You were right. I can do this. And now I believe I can do anything.'"

So if you have had any success at all, it could give you confidence that you can have more. You learn to run and win or pass a hard math exam or operate a camera or make a painting in 30 minutes. Maybe you can next pivot from your present job or start a new career. At least try or you'll never know how you'll do. Spend a few hours studying your past interests, where you stand out, what you are good at. It's a project to confront these decisions. But it couldn't be for a better cause: your own happiness and bank account.

Maybe between Bob and Chyna, we should all watch more television to bump into ideas for new careers. Or be more open to change as we live our normal lives. But ideas are only the beginning. You have to execute. You have to persist. You have to work hard: it's no easy step from wanting to have your own TV show to launching it just two years later. Some of it may be luck, but lots of circumstances must come together for it to work out so well.

Both people had talents, had some skills or distinctive traits. They also weren't limited by their histories and previous careers.

Jack Gilpin started acting in TV shows and movies in 1968, when he was 17. He has since been in dozens of film and stage productions and is still having a satisfying career. I saw him in the movie, *Trouble with the Curve*, but I missed his recurring performances over the years in *Kate & Allie* and *Law & Order*.

Jack grew up as an Episcopalian and was confirmed when he was 12. But for the next 20 years, he didn't have much to do with his religion and its ritual. Then suddenly, he felt a strong spiritual need to return to his faith. This drive was so strong that he even chose to attend school to earn his Master of Divinity degree, which is normally a three-year program. One advantage of his acting career was that he was not fully employed all the time, so he could fit in the classes between projects. After seven years, at age 37, Jack completed the courses and became a lay preacher. All while still acting. In fact, one job took him out of state to California for a month. He had a friend record the lectures and send them to him. He arranged to take his tests on location. I wonder if his fellow actors had any idea what Jack was doing off the set, when they were hanging out and having a good time. However, Jack was determined. He made his dream a reality.

**Jack Gilpin, Easter Sunday 2017.
Photo by Flora Quammie.**

Another time he portrayed a priest in a movie filmed in

Hoboken, New Jersey. During shooting breaks, he could see people in the streets spotting his collar from a distance and noticed how their body language changed, drooping and no eye contact. Maybe it was from guilt or being reminded they were sinners. Jack felt it didn't have to be like that. People should feel glad to see their spiritual leader. He wanted to be that comforting person.

Jack says that nothing was missing from his acting profession. He simply 'saw how life was and that it was articulated in the church.' It spoke to him. He also had time in between acting jobs and wanted to do more with that time.

Now he is the rector of St John's Episcopal Church in New Milford, Connecticut. He was ordained a priest in December 2012 and said he can't believe he has an office and a congregation. In 2016, I bumped into his performances in two episodes on TV of *Billions*. He had integrated his parish responsibilities and his acting life.

How is that for a reinvention? Or would you call it a pivot? Or an expansion? Whatever your term, Jack has to be applauded for taking 31 years, from age 30 to 61, to alter how he lives his life, relates to and serves other people. He is certainly an inspiration to us all.

Nevertheless. I do everything in my power to defeat him, when we are on opposite sides of the tennis court. Even if he has God on his team.

Reinvention can take all forms.

I remember Michael Rosen, a college roommate, who studied electrical engineering, became a computer programmer, but decided he liked taking pictures more. Eventually he became an art photographer specializing in photos of 'radical, healthy sexuality.' He published books and had many gallery exhibitions. Who would have guessed that is how he would have reinvented himself? Although Michael doesn't use that word. He says he, "found what he was always supposed to do." Since he became a professional photographer in 1977, he worked part time jobs in the computer field to supplement his income.

Michael's wife, Lucille Lannan, graduated college with a business degree and coordinated travel for people at the United Nations. In college, she had typed papers for money to pay for Berlitz School Spanish classes that helped secure her UN job. However, she always wanted to be a lawyer. So she and her husband moved to Washington, DC, where she worked as a secretary in a law office. For three full years including summers, she took night classes at George Washington University to earn her law degree and then spent almost all her 40-year law career at the National Labor Relations Board in California.

This whole idea of changing careers when you are older and established in another pursuit is very challenging to accomplish. We all need money to survive. Learning a new field at night, while you still have income from your day job, is the least stressful way to make the switch.

If your day-job disappears, because you are in an accident or are fired or the company shuts down, then you'll need to change careers suddenly. I hope you have some savings or grants to give you full-time to learn new skills or have already acquired them along the way. Dancers can teach, athletes can also become TV announcers. But what can you do is the only question you probably care about.

I remember being painfully embarrassed decades ago, when I was in the elevator of a New York department store, and the operator in his uniform said hello to me. It took me seconds to recognize a former art director in a big ad agency who had been let go when his company was contracting during a recession. It would have been nice for him to have had a Plan B before he was fired. But this was a good warning for me. Those ad agencies did become more productive: they reduced the number of employees they had on staff for each million dollars of billings from maybe 10 down to five.

Sometimes the reason you need to find a new career has nothing to do with being fired. Barbara was a successful and respected cellist who performed with orchestras at Carnegie Hall, on Broadway, at the Kennedy Center. One day in 1985, picking up music at Newark's Symphony Hall, she fell three floors down the shaft of a stage lift that had been removed. Her back was broken in two places, and her music career was over. It was just too demanding physically to practice, perform, move her beloved cello around. Tragic. She was 32.

During her recovery and therapy, she began to take one literature course at a time at Hunter College in Manhattan. She wrote about it in *Allegro* in June, 1998: "I progress from using the walker, to metal crutches that wrap around my arms, to two canes, and then one. In class I wear my back brace and lie down periodically on a thick mat at the side of the room. I take notes there, lying on my back."

With unwavering determination, she obtained a scholarship and completed a number of undergraduate courses that weren't required for her music degrees. Then she decided to pursue her love of literature and attended the City of

New York (CUNY) graduate center. She received a super fellowship, which pays for tuition, books and living expenses. She studied for eight years and earned two additional master's degrees and a PhD in English literature.

Her doctoral dissertation consumed two of those years and described musical orchestration in Wallace Stevens' poetry. (It's especially fitting to point out that Stevens worked his last 40 years as an insurance executive in Hartford, CT. I read that he sometimes conceived his poetry while walking to and from his office. He is another example, like Jack Gilpin, of how to integrate two dissimilar careers into one life.)

In 1994, Barbara joined the English department at the CUNY/ LaGuardia campus, where she taught and published articles for 22 years, rising to full professor. She helped create and teach innovative programs that incorporated music, art and philosophy of art into a new Creativity Cluster.

In that same 1998 article about her transition, she says, "I find that I absorb poetry in the same way as I comprehend music. *When reading a poem, I savor the feel of the words in my mouth.* Like music, poetry is kinetic, tactile.

Both alter our emotions, our very consciousness, through bodily sensations." Her words are like music to my eyes. Beautiful.

It's easy to imagine how disappointing and heartbreaking Barbara's forced change would be for anyone. Much more difficult to feel the pain of those first post-accident steps, the endless hours of therapy. How many would just vegetate and live with self-pity and sadness? She sure deserves our admiration for her fortitude and accommodation—taking notes in the classroom, while lying on a mat. Wow! That is grit, tenacity, guts, heart and spunk!!!

I would never state in this case that if she can do it, you can do it. But of the 123 million full-time workers in the United States, I am sure there ARE millions who have changed their careers and learned to earn money in new and different ways. Some more than once. All that matters to you is that you join those in the smaller group who are successful in shifting their income source. Or find greater fulfillment. And go to work enthusiastically.

You only need the confidence to think you might be part of that smaller group that can do it. You have to figure out how to get from where you are to the next spot on your road. You have to put in the hundreds of hours necessary to acquire new skills and knowledge. You have to have the courage to apply for the job, send out your resume, risk rejection in an interview.

The process is so clear. And if you make the effort and fail completely, then at least you are no worse off than if you hadn't tried at all. But I really don't believe that. All your work and new contacts and changed view of yourself is sure to lead to some alteration in the route you are taking after you have sought your new dream.

Sometimes opportunities fall into your lap. You just need to pivot a bit in your current field, like Heather Taylor did.

She began in the fashion industry in New York City, but decided in 2011 to return to Miami and become an actress. She was successful in being hired as an extra, stand-in and photo double in some TV shows, such as *Magic City*, *Graceland* and *Burn Notice*. One difficulty is that an extra in Miami only earns $112 gross for 12 hours of work. (It may be

$172 for a SAG member who works eight hours in NYC.)

People work as extras for all kinds of reasons: fun, money, learning to become an actor. Heather did it for networking and to gain experience. A friend of mine tried it once but couldn't stand that they had to be on set at 5 am, so he left three hours later.

Then Florida changed its tax incentives for production companies. This was a major loss for the industry. A significant new trend. The kind you want to pay attention to, and I devote a whole chapter to later. Anyway, Florida jobs in the film field dried right up.

Heather moved to Atlanta, where her best friend lived, and the exact opposite trend in the production business was underway. Atlanta was growing big time in the TV/film area, and is now the third largest production center in the US, after NY and LA. Relocating to where the jobs are is a very big decision. Many people are too settled and unwilling to change their habits. Can you relate to that inertia?

On the drive up, Heather made calls to casting directors and spoke to one she had worked through in Miami. He offered her a casting job working with him, but she turned him down.

After a while, when extra jobs were not happening for her in Atlanta, she changed her mind, took the casting position and basically taught herself, because her boss wasn't always there. She had switched careers in November 2013. Less than two years later, she went off on her own.

Now in her early thirties, she is the casting director of her own company, finding talent for movies and TV shows. It's called Casting TaylorMade. She now has an assistant and has worked with Tyler Perry's TV shows, *The Front Runner* movie starring Hugh Jackman, *The Immortal Life of Henrietta Lacks* for HBO with Oprah, and *Stranger Things* for Netflix, where she was part of the team that WON an Emmy for best casting in a drama series. She has a real hands-on approach, only accepts one or two projects at a time, and works side-by-side with the director. She has done all the different jobs, knows what is needed, and is working 12 hours a day to make her business grow.

Heather Taylor

She has no regrets about pivoting her role in the industry. She now not only has more money, but more money more consistently. Now she is the person giving out the parts, rather than the person looking for them. Thriving. Loves what she is doing. Has real determination and perseverance.

It is a great expansion of her talents, different ones than being an actress or an extra. She gave that side of the field a try, and discovered that she could really make a difference in an unexpected role. And she took that chance, made that jump. Seems perfectly logical in hindsight. But even she didn't say yes right away.

Heather is lucky that the casting director who offered her the position as his assistant didn't fill it by the time Heather called him back. Very fortunate. We all know friends or movie characters who had the chance to take a new position, buy a house, accept a dinner invitation but declined and regretted that decision. Did that ever happen to you? Slow down the next time you have an opportunity. Think about it carefully if it involves your career. You never know where saying 'Yes" can alter your path for the rest of your life.

Malena is a South American woman who cleans houses for her living. She has been doing it for 19 years. She is trustworthy and thorough, two traits of value to people who have weekend homes and are giving the cleaning people keys to their doors. Well, word got around, and after a while, there was more work than one human could handle. So, a friend was brought in, then another, and another. People need to have their houses cleaned. Right? Especially weekenders who want to arrive Friday night and find beds made from last visit, emptied trash cans, laundered towels and sheets.

Can you tell where this is heading? Malena and her cleaning crew are performing a valuable service. She offered trust and a thoroughness that her clients were willing to pay for. Most days she leaves for her first house at 7am and doesn't return until 8 pm. She checks the houses that her employees clean to make sure they are perfect. She charges her clients more than she pays her team, so Malena makes additional dollars each week. She speaks English well enough to avoid language misunderstandings with the homeowners not fluent in Spanish. A real win-win for everyone. A win-win win, because there are now three parties involved.

It sounds like such an obvious pivot and extension of a basic capability. But the other maids working for her didn't do it. Or couldn't. Or were afraid. Or didn't have self-confidence. And building up a larger business is a very different skill set than just one person serving 10-15 clients each week.

Even better, she and her husband Jose save their money to invest. They bought a piece of land years ago in Peru for $18,000. Since then, they turned down an offer to sell it for $200,000. In six to seven years, Jose tells me he will be able to divide the 99 acres into lots and sell them individually for a million dollars. This will be their retirement fund.

A fabulous success story built on hard work and a willingness to expand or pivot as the situation demands. When they first came to America and tried telemarketing in Florida, they didn't like it or think it had potential. So, after eight months they moved to Connecticut. Malena was a nanny and maid. Jose started at the bottom doing landscaping and learned all the skills necessary to eventually have his own contracting business offering carpentry and painting.

No one is going to hand you anything. Some might applaud, cheer, support your vision. Others will tell you to give up a stupid dream that is not attainable, is not sensible, does not have much hope. It is a very emotional battle. You must fight. But not to show others you could succeed. Rather, because it is your dream, and you want to make it happen and are willing to put in the hours, deal with, and solve the setbacks. The more you stick with it and refine it, the more enthusiasm you have for it, then the more you will meet others who do respect your effort and will be helpful and open doors for you.

Millions of people start out on one road and end up somewhere along another. But only those walking or jogging will ever reach a great distance along the way. Just wave to those bystanders in beach chairs under umbrellas with sun glasses and iced drinks. They ain't goin' nowhere. Years of not thinking about change, makes it harder to ever do any change.

But you can do it. It just takes some *ganas*. Some desire. Some motivation. Some smarts to see a need or opportunity in the market and a huge effort that will be worth it in ways you could never foresee.

CHAPTER THREE

NEVER GIVE UP

In 2004, I wrote an Op Ed about political bigotry, urging Republicans and Democrats to find middle ground. *The New York Times* and *Wall Street Journal* rejected it as well as most other major national papers.

I decided to make a list of the 100 biggest-circulation papers in the country and started sending it out, one at a time. By the 47th rejection, I was running out of hope. That is when I heard from the *Seattle Times*, which bought my article. When the article was published, I enjoyed comments from very supportive readers. I also set a good example for my 14 and 15-year-old kids: sticking with a goal might pay off—never give up. Being persistent applies to all arenas, whether making money, changing jobs or careers, searching for friends and lovers, focusing on good health, seeking happiness.

When I was a publisher training people how to sell advertising space in my magazines, I told employees that if you call 100 people, you will find 10 who might be interested. From those 10 you have a good chance of finding one buyer. You can't succeed by just calling 10 or 20 prospects. You must keep at it.

When I asked the head of sales for the giant publishing house Simon & Schuster how many of his books made money, he said, "If 888 books were published, 800 would lose money, 80 would break even, and eight would bring in all the money to make the whole company profitable." But he didn't always know which were the big eight. The authors with the real winners wouldn't come to you, unless you had a big list each year. The rewards result from continuing to aim for winners. The key was to stay with it and not to stop too soon.

When I was in the tableware field, I learned that only one or two patterns made all the money from the plate designs offered or all the silverware styles in some of the country's most famous companies. However, companies had to keep trying different ones, until they identified the ones that lots of people wanted.

The venture capital field, works on the same principle. The analysts who spend full time researching young companies, and doing all the due diligence with the help of skilled staffers and number crunchers, only pick a tiny percent of all the small companies they have reviewed. Yet, four to six out of 10 of those selected will lose every dime invested. Three to four will break even. And one–maybe two–will win big enough to offset all the losses, all the office expenses, and make VC principals super rich.

That's how hard it is to succeed in an investment field full of smart guys who have millions to invest in companies so small that they have minimal revenues, less than 10 people employed, and may be on the verge of bankruptcy. Very high risk.

Venture capitalists don't know which companies are the winners. Thus, they keep on trying until they get the big score. If they are lucky and smarter more often than not, they will succeed. Imagine: only one or possibly two out of 10 companies will make money for VC investors out of the hundreds or thousands that were considered, and that's before those final 10 were chosen.

Do you want to be the best baseball pitcher or artist or musician or snowboarder? Do you have enough talent to do so? The least you can do is find out? Put it all out there, and give it everything you've got. Lay it all on the mat – like they told me in my aikido class.

There is a famous juggler named, Michael Moschen. He told me he worked on a skill involving crystal glass balls maybe two inches in diameter. He practiced two years before he could move those balls through and around his fingers with such grace and beauty that it's been called balletic art. He certainly never gave up. Two years!

I remember this one neighborhood kid in my high school band who spent all his time practicing the trumpet. I'd be playing in the street or riding my bike, and Eddie Masur's magic melodies would serenade the air. It was beautiful. I can still hear him in my head right now.

I was a trumpet player in the band as well, and I couldn't stand practicing those fight songs and chromatic scales. I always felt guilty that he was putting in the time, and I wasn't. No surprise, I was last seat playing the third trumpet parts, and Eddie was second seat playing the first trumpet parts. No surprise he was determined. He practiced. He didn't give up. And he achieved results that I didn't.

Maybe I didn't have any musical talent, and no matter how hard I practiced, I would never end up floating with the cream in that milk bottle. But practicing and trying harder would have probably moved me higher. An alternative plan is to NEVER GIVE UP, and to search for a field you like and that you can't wait to play and practice in.

Tennis turned out to be one of those places for me. Who knew? When I was 12 and 13, I went to a brief tennis clinic run by Gardnar Mulloy, who won five Grand Slam doubles tournaments. I won the clinic one year and was runner-up another. But I never kept at it. I was too busy earning money from the time I was nine, delivering newspapers after school.

When I semi-retired at age 67, I finally had more time. I started playing again; sometimes five hours a day and two to five times a week. I had many bad habits when swinging a racket. I knew what I should be doing, but my body just wasn't doing it. I was jealous of adults who had been honing their skills for decades. I meet men who have 40 to 70 years of playing behind them.

So, I what did I do? Practice, practice, practice. I can't get enough of it. I stay with it. I am often the player in doubles who encourages a disheartened more skilled partner to perk up even when we are losing. Once I was playing doubles, and we were behind in a tiebreaker, where we needed seven points for victory, and we were losing 0-5. My partner had all but given up, but there I was pumping him up. I saw I was getting him to rally. I saw a spark fire inside him, and we won seven points in a row. Stay with it. Keep fighting.

One good bit of advice I heard is that practice makes perfect, however, that is only true if YOU ARE PRACTICING PERFECTLY! It doesn't help to hit 1000 balls the wrong way. That's not the muscle memory you want to instill in your neurons. So, take lessons, read books, watch videos, have videos taken of yourself.

It's ridiculous to think anyone can become good at something right away. I have to work at tennis constantly, read about mental techniques, play in games, overcome fears and anxieties. How else does one achieve growth, improvement and the satisfaction of hitting a winning shot past a threatening opponent?

This is all so obvious, when I describe a tennis stroke. So why isn't it clear in any other pursuit? You can't write a great article the first time you try or repair car engines after a week of watching someone else. It takes research scientists years in some cases to find a gene or bacterium they were searching for. And you don't become the boss just two years after joining a firm. In Japan, it used to take five years as an apprentice making by hand the glob of rice that the raw fish is placed on, before one could advance to sushi chef. That's too long for me.

But you get the idea. It's so easy to understand. Disregard it, and you are in trouble on your road to money, success and happiness.

I learned recently about the early story of a book called *Chicken Soup for the Soul*.[4] I'd heard of the title, but didn't know that there are 250 books in the series that have sold 500 million copies. "That first book, which had been rejected by 144 publishers, went on to sell 10 million copies," writes co-author Jack Canfield.[5]

Can you imagine how hard it is to receive 144 rejections? The pain he felt? Well how about the pain felt by all those "smart" publishers who rejected the book? And the small publisher who did accept it thought it would sell just 25,000 copies, even though the authors came with pre-orders of 20,000 copies from their self-help workshops. Amazing!

But Margaret Mitchell endured at least 18 rejections, before her *Gone with the Wind* was accepted. And *Catcher in the*

Rye sold 80 million copies after it had been rejected as well.

I also discovered other notable rejections:

The book *M.A.S.H*—21 times; *Zen and the Art of Motorcycle Maintenance*—121 times. *Dr. Seuss*—23 times; Stephen King's *Carrie*—30 times, *The Naked and the Dead*—20 times. And the list goes on and on and on.

Good thing these authors didn't give up, and that they believed in their manuscripts, and kept going despite the incorrect assessments of "experts." I believe there are thousands of success stories that resulted after failure and rejection. But their creators would not accept defeat, whether new inventions, performance artists, actors and models, start-up businesses...or people just looking to be: hired, have a date with an appealing person, travel to a foreign country, earn a better grade, stop smoking... anything.

Best lesson to learn of all is that you can't swim in the pond if you don't jump in. You must be in the Game of Life, if you ever want to win. And once you are playing, and heading towards the light on the other side, you might discover that you modify your goal, you change your path—or it shifts by winds and waves you don't control—and you end up somewhere you never imagined or knew about.

That's a big part of the adventure. It can be thrilling. It is full of surprises. And I believe very few people, if any, know in advance exactly how their lives are going to evolve. So just start from wherever you are on your journey. It's not like you have a choice, because you can't go back–at least not until someone (you maybe?) invents a time machine...

Talking about swimming reminds me of Jessica Tatiana

Long,[6] who has twice won the ESPY Award for the best female athlete with a disability. She is the second most decorated Paralympian in US history, has held and holds many records for Paralympic events, and has won 23 Paralympic medals (including 13 golds), all in swimming.

When she was 18 months, both her lower legs were amputated, and she has artificial legs that enable her to be a model and cheerleader, and compete in gymnastics, ice skating, biking, and rock climbing. One of her mottos in life is to "Never (never, never) give up," which was delivered originally by Sir Winston Churchill.

Born in Russia, but adopted at 13 months by Americans who raised her in Baltimore, she is an astonishing inspiration and a supreme example of how fickle life can be. With all the odds against her at the start, and with the support of loving step-parents, she has transformed herself into a success in many areas no one could have ever imagined. Maybe that is true for you. You never know. At the very least, keep at it, whatever "it" is for you.

I saw a documentary called, *The Other Shore* about Diana Nyad,[7] a competitive distance swimmer who swam around Manhattan (28 miles), when she was 26. Four years later she swam 102 miles from The Bahamas to Florida, an open water world record. Then she stopped swimming competitively for 31 years!

However, she had this goal to be the first person to swim from Cuba to Key West, Florida, without a shark cage, 110 miles. Why did she take on this challenge after three decades?

"Because I'd like to prove to the other 60-year-olds that it is never too late to start your dreams."

After five tries, between 2010 and 2013, she finally did it. She swam for 53 hours. The film shows the pain and struggle of fighting currents, soreness, horrible jellyfish stings, and what seemed like her near death, when she had to be yelled at to breathe in and breathe out after failing at one of the attempts.

She was never a "normal" person, for she had set many swimming records in her youth and was also a top squash player. Yet her determination and will to succeed, despite four crushingly disappointing failures, is on display in her story.

I would never say that if Diana can do it, then you or I can do it. But I will promise that not giving up right away, giving the effort another try, believing that you might reach your goal are very powerful. I am also sure that if you can create the will, you will encounter hidden, unknown powers inside of yourself that you never knew about and that you can use in all aspects of your daily life. Never give up—instead give it another attempt.

CHAPTER FOUR

EASIER WAYS TO MAKE MONEY THAN YOU WERE EVER TAUGHT IN SCHOOL

It's no secret that most people want to make more money... and that many self-help books focus on how you can acquire more of that green power to buy things. There are countless tales of how money doesn't buy happiness, you can live on love alone, poor people are happier than rich people.

However, I think those are dishonest rationalizations. You should ignore all those movies and books showing rich people who are unhappy, pathetic or morosely drunk, or even suicidal and blaming it on too much money. Being rich or poor, you can be happy or miserable. But almost everyone will agree it's better to be well fed, to cry on a clean–if not silk–pillow, have roomy, pleasant shelter and to have many other material possessions for playing, wearing etc. Life experiences like vacations aren't so bad either.

How do you typically acquire money?

Obviously, you can work for it. Some people receive $15 an hour for basic, relatively unskilled manual labor. Usually an education will allow you to charge more for your time. Plumbers and electricians charge $100. Lawyers and accountants can earn $600 an hour or more for knowledge and expertise.

I am not talking now about the billionaires like Larry Ellison, whose enormous wealth generates $38,000 an hour, per one *New York Times Magazine* article. Hey, he's one of the 10 richest people in the world.

I am referring to people who make their money by putting in the hours and who keep a Time Sheet and charge their clients an agreed-upon amount for each time unit expended.

There are consultants and commercial photographers who charge a daily rate, regardless of whether they work eight or 15 hours. And then there are most people, who earn an annual wage, say $30,000 or $100,000-plus a year for their time chopped up into weekly or half-monthly payments.

If they are lucky, and their companies or bosses do well, these annual-earning laborers might receive a bonus and some perks, like use of a company car or some free meals that will reduce their expenses.

We are usually taught that obtaining a 'good' job is one of the goals of labor, and the more skills you have or education you received will give you a huge edge up in being hired for that desirable job. For most of us mere mortals, however, it's a no-win situation for making big money.

Not knowing any better, I went that route, and prayed for my annual raise or 'thank you' bonus. I often felt I was underpaid, that my boss didn't appreciate me, that I should have been awarded more. But it's a losing fight, because the only leverage you have is threatening to leave. Until you take that risk, the boss or his boss wants to pay you as little as possible.

I worked in that game for 12 years. Very frustrating. One time after I was fired in a recession, where I had been earning $32,000 a year, the only job I could find was in a large, established company for $26,000. My new boss said that if I proved myself, he'd do what he could to bring me closer to what I used to earn.

Months later, after I'd made major contributions to our department, I found a better job. But I thought I'd see how sincere my current boss was and if he'd keep his word. I asked for a raise, even though I had no intention of staying, and a few days later I was told 10% ($2600) was the best he could do. However, he'd persuaded top management to increase it to $3000. That wasn't even close to what he had promised. Plus, he presented it like I should be eternally grateful. This was a 100-year-old company, he reminded me, with over 1000 employees. There were rules, and changing them was impossible.

In one of the most satisfying moments of my career up to that point, I said, "Well that's a real shame. I quit!" I gave him two-week's notice. He was stunned, shaken. He really counted on me. I had increased his department's revenues and accomplishments significantly, compared to the 8-10 others who were less ambitious.

Two days later he called me into his office with a proud smile and told me that if I stayed, I could receive a $10,000 raise. He'd found the money from somewhere. I told him I'd think about it, and wondered how I was going let him down gently. $36,000 a year was more than I was to be paid at my next company, which produced ads, events and publicity for the Nikon camera company. I left anyway.

It was quite the lesson. It's often a negotiation, but the poor employee usually has less advantages.

What else can you do? How about commission income, where you receive a percentage of everything you sell? This has more potential sometimes. If you're really good, you will sell more and make more. Often your company will give you an 'advance each week against those commissions,' but as soon as you aren't producing enough sales, whether they are cars or jet engines, you are fired and looking for another job. It's a risk.

You hear stories about the IBM computer salesman, Ross Perot, who sold his yearly quota and earned his year's commission in the first two weeks of January. After his unusual ideas were ignored by his superiors, he left to start his own computer software company, became a billionaire and ran for President of the United States—TWICE! But most sales types aren't that gifted or set up in a situation where they can make a killing and earn a year's income in two weeks. I think you have to stop looking at those public examples of humongous success and think you can do it too. It's very unlikely. Though they may inspire you, their stories might also depress you, when you accept that you are not as talented or lucky as they are. You should be realistic.

Another way to obtain money is to create something tangible from nothing, which is what painters, writers, and sculptors do. They take huge chances. Some of these artists make big money or know how to market, even hype, their output. But most don't make much at all. However, they also don't enter these creative fields with the main goal of making money. They just have a need to do their art. They may have demons that need to be expressed in some artistic medium. This is similar to actors, musicians and singers, but these creatives are initially offering labor and talent, not some physical product, although the music makers can then sell recordings. What they all usually have in common is passion, which is very important for your success. Do you have any passions?

I published a book about avant garde art. I learned that less than 2% of artists in America—and these are old statistics—earn enough money from their art to support themselves. But if you are driven to create, you really have no choice. If you are a painter, you do have to find time, space, materials. You need money, which is something most artists have little talent managing. To you I say find a knowledgeable friend or relative and heed what you hope is sound business advice. Especially if you know that you are not so skilled making decisions involving money.

Now, I want to show you how normal people can make bigger, non-salary money. First, most of us don't work for Google or Facebook, where secretaries and low-level employees receive stock early on and end up as millionaires. You have to look for more likely ways than those lucky winners. Most companies are not start-ups, and most start-ups won't have that kind of track record. Forget about them for now, because almost all of them go out of business! Nevertheless, I will talk in detail about start-ups in a separate chapter.

Here is the most important advice I can state: making money by selling your labor is not the best way to earn serious or retirement money. The ideal approach is to invest money in something else that will earn money for you, whether it's stocks, real estate, your own store, your own business. Obvious, right? Not to most people.

I say that because you need money to achieve these goals, and most people don't have extra money to invest. In fact, they spend so much that they are in debt to the bank, credit card companies, organizations that loan money at exorbitant rates. And once you are submerged in that quicksand of debt, it's almost impossible to free yourself and live unencumbered by that burden.

When I grew up, I felt poor compared to some around me, although our family was considered lower middle class. I had classmates in high school being given cars or new wardrobes every year, and one rich girl received a hotel for her 16th birthday! I was delivering newspapers from my bicycle by age 9 and worked after school as a cabana boy, soda jerk and carpenter's helper. I knew how hard it was to earn money, and I valued every bit of it.

While in the Army, I made $200 a month plus some parachute jump pay and hardship pay for being stationed overseas. I was only 21, when I started my two years of service, and when I was done I had saved $5000. Even back then, I knew that it took money to make money.

I certainly wasn't the guy buying rounds of drinks at the bar every night. I didn't spend lavishly on clothes, didn't own a car for years, rarely spent wildly on pleasures that others took for granted.

Now, if you are over 30 and in debt already, you have a tough challenge. If you are married with kids and have one of those 'good jobs,' it's very hard to save money. I know, because I see it all around me and have noticed the pattern for decades. People want to be liked and respected. Thus, they buy cars they can't afford, clothes that are costly (and maybe soon out of fashion), and live in fancy apartments or houses beyond their means to impress their friends or others with upscale addresses. In my opinion, they do not have a vision for their future. They can't look ahead and see how they are digging themselves into a pit of debt. They also can't see that having a stash of cash might make them comfortable enough to risk a significant portion of that nest egg and even totally lose a small part of it.

If you want big rewards, you must take big risks. If you play it safe–because you can't afford to lose any of it, because you have so little of it–then you will have unimpressive returns and never build up that big reserve of funds for those rainy or future days.

Doesn't this all sound obvious? Of course it does. But saving money is a huge challenge and achievement. Many people can do it if they have some big goal in mind, like buying a new car or a house. But, without that plan and the determination to make it real for you, it's a mountain too high to climb for most individuals.

I am hoping to convince you that you must start now, whether you are young or old. If you have debts already, you need to reduce them. Deprive yourself for a while, give up some treats, some expensive vacations or any long vacation. It's only for a short period. Keep the benefit of accumulating a pile of money (no matter how small) at the front of your mind. Maybe take a second job. Resist the demands of your non-working spouse/significant other to spend your money for you. If he/she isn't supportive, do everything you can to explain the upcoming benefits. Every time you reduce debt, you are reducing those usurious interest payments.

I knew someone with $55,000 of credit card debt who was paying $10,000 a year in interest. He could never rid himself of that debt, because he could barely afford to pay the interest. That's a rate of around 20%, when banks are lending money at 3-5%. Madness. I was paying my mortgage interest at a rate less than 3%. But he was careless in earlier years and spent money foolishly. He leased the nicer car for an extra $150 a month, for example. Not ideal.

Let's be optimistic and assume you either have debt you can eliminate or no debt at all. Now you must be disciplined, beyond anything you can imagine, keep your day job, and start saving. You must build up a cache of cash that you are willing to invest: a small portion in higher risk places, the bulk in medium risk ventures, and a third portion in safer vehicles.

Remember always that the house can wait, and so can a prestigious car. At one point, I bought an old VW for $40 and started my publishing business, while driving that bug 20,000 miles. I did splurge on a new, cheap paint job. But I also had wire holding down the fender. Too radical for you? I had no one to impress. I was determined to take advantage of my rare chance to become free of bosses who could fire me again.

After a few years pass, you will be ready to begin. Where do you invest?

Most people reading this might be tempted by the idea of owning their own business that sells products from a retail store. Common but hard and risky. Especially these years, when on-line retailing (like Amazon) is undercutting every local store. You better have a good product or service, one that is needed and not already supplied in your area. And you better be willing to put in far more hours and energy than in the job you currently have working for other people and companies.

I had a father-in-law who owned a restaurant. Long hours, late nights, employee thefts, even robberies. Subjected to rising food prices, changing neighborhood demographics. Had to relocate when his lease ran out. Not for me. And in my opinion, who needs another restaurant?

You just better pick a store or new business idea that excites you. If your heart and soul and mind and family aren't totally into it, you probably won't make it. Don't worry about boredom later; if it succeeds, you can hire someone else to do the jobs you did in the beginning.

One of the most common areas of investment is real estate. There are lots and lots of people who have the ability to buy a rundown building or apartment cheaply, fix it up— often with their own labor—and then rent or sell it for a profit. So many people do this that it's mind boggling. My wife's parents did this for years; in fact they would buy properties for almost nothing at auction foreclosed on by government loan programs. My mother-in-law lived in 23 different homes. As soon as she fixed one up, she sold it and bought another one to renovate and sell.

I know a father-son team that buys rural homes undervalued and flips them after doing much of the labor themselves. It's a skill to learn how much to spend on a particular residence, how much it will cost to renovate it, how much it might bring in a particular market at a specific time. But millions of people make money this way, and sometimes they make killings. It's not usually all their own money at risk: by putting down say 20-25% of the total needed, they can borrow the rest from a bank. That is why you need to have that small pile of cash to get started.

Joseph Adler

Your first small real estate venture might be an evening and weekend project, until you can do it full time. Maybe you are hiring others and watching and learning what they do. But once again: You should like it. If it's not appealing to you, if you can't stand the dirt, the noise, the uncertainty, the potential to make nothing if you underestimated your costs and the rental/sales price, then don't even consider it.

You should search hard and find something that interests you. Ideally some field that thrills you and that you can't live without.

Identifying a source of passion is one of the great blessings in a human life. It's also a gift if you find it. One of my closest friends, Joseph Adler, is in his 70s and still running a small regional theater, casting and directing plays that he finds in New York or London and that exhilarate him and his audiences. He has had this passion for the stage and film since elementary school, when I first met him. So lucky. So blessed. For my first 30 years, I envied him and others like him who were driven to be in a certain field. He knows how fortunate he is to be so enthused about his craft. He says that most people are not passionate about anything.

But most people never spend hours or years dealing with this very confronting decision. Most people do have interests, but they never imagine or figure out how they might earn a living from those interests. If you reflect and are open and bump into even the remotest tingle of excitement, then follow up with deeper exploration, talk to people in the field. At some point, hopefully, no one can stop you from reading more about it, watching videos and movies connected to your interest. You are launched.

I felt that way about photography after I stared taking pictures of my first child. I gradually realized that I wanted to be around photographers and pictures full time, and that I wanted to earn their respect. But I didn't want to be either just another great photographer, nor be a picture editor. I spent six years looking and talking to people to somehow imagine what I could do in this industry that I was drawn to. Eventually, I learned about the need for an annual promotional publication and then had to learn how to be a publisher, raise money, start and run a business, etc. By the time I was fired again, I had already started my new life on the side to publish photography books.

When that happened, I felt it was my one chance to grab the brass ring from the merry-go-round, and I worked sometimes 20 hours a day to make it a success. There were constant setbacks, surprises, annoyances and agonies. Sometimes I was terrified of failing. But that's what it's all about.

I read that of all the businesses that are started, 30% die in the first year, another 30% in the second year, and a final 30% in the third year. Only 10% survive longer than three years. That's just one of 10 start-ups. I celebrated in the midst of my fourth year. These numbers show you the odds you are facing in starting your own business. Too daunting? Can't feel passionate about any particular idea or industry.

Then don't do it. Hang on to your savings.

If it makes you feel any easier, I read in 2015 that 50% of new start-ups are still around after five years. The odds of success have increased from my beginning days in the late 70s. But those current articles also predict that only two out of 10 will survive at all. So, it's still a substantial risk. But big risk offers big rewards. Do you have the stomach for it?

I learned recently about an entrepreneur named Bill Gross[8] who had his own businesses since he was 12 years old selling candy bars. Since then he and his Idealab start -up factory have created over 125 companies, most in the technology area. Only 50 have failed, 45 went public or were acquired, seven were sold for over a billion dollars, and Bill is a super rich guy. His lectures on YouTube reveal a very exciting, optimistic view.

You have to be passionate about your idea, or you won't be able to stick it out during the rough times. The market will let you know how good (or bad) your idea is. Bill quotes Mike Tyson's words, that "Everybody has a plan, until you get punched in the face." You must adapt and be pragmatic.

Bill also says that he has hundreds of ideas for companies. They blossom out of his frustration with something in his everyday life that doesn't please him or work smoothly: he says, "there ought to be a firm or product that makes/ provides this"—and then he starts one.

His optimism arises out of his observation that through the internet and the mobile revolution, a new company can today reach seven billion cell phones. And the number of users will increase every year. That is an historically unprecedented, galactic audience to sell to or help. Have any ideas???

On the other hand, I have met many salaried people trying to come up with a great app, struggling for years to even have one good business idea, quietly resentful that I was so lucky to figure something out (after I was fired yet again). Running your own business isn't easy and it just isn't for everyone.

Fortunately, there is another major area for using money to make money, and you can enter this fray no matter how little you have.

I am referring to the public stock market. An arena in which you can buy and sell a piece of another company in seconds: totally liquid. And you can be in the game with as little money as you want to risk. It could be $50 to start. The great thing here is that if you are determined, and reasonably competent, notice trends in our society and do your research, you can make a lot of money. Stocks are an ideal place to make money from money. No labor required.

One of my friends is 75. He retired in his 40s and has made all his money since from stock investments. He said he treats it like a job and spends at least an hour every day reviewing his portfolio, reading the business news, following the global economic developments. I could never do that, but I admire his discipline and fortitude.

On the other hand, I have read many stories in the papers about the lady schoolteacher or naive-seeming librarian who dies and leaves millions to some charity all earned to everyone's astonishment from her personal stock market investments.

There was just such a story about Ronald Read in Brattleboro, VT who seemed so poor that well-meaning townspeople were buying fence wire from him they didn't need and knitting him hats, so he could be warmer in winter. With minimal education and after working at a gas station for 25 years and then at JCPenney, Read died in 2015 and left the town library and hospital $8,000,000, all accumulated from picking stocks.

Sometimes it isn't so difficult to spot a new industry worth risking some of your money in; pick the company or two in that field that has a good chance of succeeding in it. After the army, restless to increase my $5000 of savings, I spent eight months reading books, going to museums, learning how to learn, and how to invest in the stock market. I knew nothing about stocks.

I could see that Color TV was going to be valued, so I bought 10 shares of RCA. I gradually risked more of my savings as the total value grew bigger on paper. After I married and took a job, my portfolio continued to grow. At one point, I had stocks worth $21,000. My wife and I were giddy. I was proud and flying high. Back then you could buy a Jaguar for $7000. Life was good.

Then I had my comeuppance: I lost it ALL and more: $23,000. Turns out I wasn't as smart as I thought. But I didn't give up. I started over once my savings were somewhat replenished. I was completely hooked on the potential of making money by investing.

I liked stocks that were offering new technological innovations, like CD ROMs. There were many I didn't appreciate and missed profiting from, even after I met the founders of Netscape and Sprint. But overall my stock investments have gone up, despite all the failures and losses. I have also decided that a professional money manager who spends his full time thinking about the stock market and the economy is worth the 1-2% fees he charges to make those key decisions of which companies to invest in and when to buy and sell. And you can also choose mutual funds and index funds. Learn about them and commit. You can do it.

To help build up your savings account for investing at all, there are many other ways to make extra money on a smaller scale. Two men I know buy cars that need work, repair them when they have time, and sell them at a profit. Both had full-time jobs, while they were fixing cars, which they love and have a real knack for. One has bought and sold over 200 cars, while he works in his family's restaurant. The other graduated from college with a music degree and decided to work instead in high performance car restoration shops. Go with what thrills you.

I know people who have passions collecting things. Maybe their collections will be worth something someday. Who knows? I would say these are not sure returns, nothing I would recommend as investments. But they are fun to find and acquire. One had hundreds of salt and pepper shakers. Another has special blue-patterned antique dishes from the 18th century. My ex-wife scours shops for a special kind of pottery called majolica. Some people have rare trains. And another friend has hundreds of various sized cheeseburgers (her favorite food) made out of plastic or metal and used as clocks, phones, earrings, paperweights, etc. Could be simply an unusual interest or maybe someday she sells these little macs for big bucks.

Buying and selling other objects like old furniture are more probable pursuits for making money in the short and medium term. I have a friend who scours antique shops and sells good finds on eBay for a quick profit. He started this on the side and now does it full time. He even has his own store now. I read about a man who specializes in pin ball machines he finds and sells on eBay as well. A neighbor likes circus paraphernalia. He has even acquired a merry-go-round. All to be sold at a higher price than purchased.

These are ways to build up extra money or start new careers. I am suggesting you also consider strategies that offer much bigger returns. And that can only result from investing.

I once bought a yellow Ferrari as an investment, when stocks and real estate were going down. It was a perfect car. I never drove it after I bought it. It's called a trailer queen—you just haul it to car shows and take home a medal without dirtying it up. But I feared tying up so much money in one object that could be damaged somehow. Within a year and a half, I sold it at auction and was thrilled to make over $150,000. Three years later it was resold for $600,000 more than I was paid. Nine years after that similar models trade for two million more than I received. Finding rare objects and holding them while they appreciate is another place to have big returns. But don't buy when there is a bubble. Or think the prices will rise forever.

Ferrari models like mine were valued in the 90s at one million dollars and then that market crashed, and for 10 years they stayed as low as $250,000. I jumped in after they started rising back up. I know a man who bought a rare Aston Martin for $27,000 and sold it 30 years later for over $3 million.

Fine art is a great investment, if you have the patience to wait for the appreciation. I bought a photograph in the 1970s for $150 by a famous fine art photographer, Harry Callahan. There were only five he had sold of the same image, and he told me all the others were in museums. Now it's worth around $20,000. But before I bought, I had learned a lot about fine art photography: I had run the Nikon photo gallery, helped start a fine art photography tabloid magazine, been to many photo exhibits, had a business partner who owned a gallery.

It's easiest and wisest to learn in depth about one special area that you know something about already, are comfortable with, that excites you, and then make your investments in that field. Cars, real estate, art, jewelry are actual objects, not like stocks, which are just small pieces of companies that are represented on a paper stock certificate or monthly statement. You can use real objects and enjoy looking at them. Even 3-D reproductions of cheeseburgers. But it takes research to discover what you like, what you can afford and what might appreciate over the years.

When I bought my Ferrari, there were others that would have cost millions. I didn't have anywhere near that much, so I looked for months to find one I admired, thought would appreciate and could afford. Even then I discovered it was nerve-wracking to have so much of my net worth tied up in one single asset. Way too much for my peace of mind, so I sold it soon after. However, I did take the chance and learned something about my dollar limits and tolerance for risk. This is different for everyone, but you need to know where your comfort level lies.

Rob Ober

Rob Ober, an art dealer I trust, grew up in Moscow, where his father was a diplomat. He returned to the States with some paintings, took a job teaching, opened the Ober Gallery with money earned giving tennis lessons, and attracted other artists. He thinks he has identified a promising, hopefully undervalued group of Russian painters classified as producing "non-conformist art." My wife and I bought a couple of their paintings thinking they may appreciate over time, like my photograph. Until then they would add beauty to our lives. But first we did a good bit of research about Russian art. We knew nothing.

A friend who is a mortgage banker likes an American painter and follows all his shows and output. He has bought maybe five or 10 over the years. When he's needed some extra funds, he's sold a painting or two at a huge profit.

It's not impossible to make money this way. Just don't expect to have results like Peggy Guggenheim,[9] who ran a modern art gallery and then bought abstractionist and expressionistic paintings for almost nothing, before the art market had accepted them. I read that in 1940 she spent $40,000 to go to Paris where she bought 10 Picassos, 40 Ernsts, 8 Miros, 4 Magrittes, 3 Man Rays, 3 Dalis, one Klee, one Chagall among others. This was just before the Germans invaded France. Now, just one of these works might be worth millions. You never know, maybe you can find art that will appreciate significantly.

By the way, although Peggy was an heiress, she gave up buying expensive couture clothing, so she would have more money for art. Sound familiar? You should cut your expenses, reduce your debt, save some funds, and then choose your investment venue.

Always be prepared to lose all or some of it. That is why you need to have enough to afford that risk.

CHAPTER FIVE

JOINING GROUPS TO ADVANCE YOUR CAREER

How far would you go to achieve career and social success? Some individuals will go to almost any lengths to be promoted, invited to the big event, or included in a special group. They don't hesitate to take steps that are devious, immoral or illegal.

Social acceptance is one of the basic needs described by Abraham Maslow, a psychologist who developed an understanding of human development and actions in western cultures. He even created a hierarchy of needs.

After people have their basic physical requirements met (food, shelter, clothing, water), they then need safety from accidents and violence, good health, and job/financial security.

Love is next, from close connections with family, friends, a spouse, a mentor. Then there is the need to belong to groups, such as clubs, co-workers, religious bodies, professional organizations, sports teams, and gangs.

I am sure you don't just desire, but really want financial security and advancement? What about belonging to groups that will help you make more money? How much are you willing to do and become and compromise to make headway toward these goals?

Obviously, millions of people choose jobs and careers that do not have money as the main priority. Think of dancers, teachers, nurses, puppeteers, and hundreds of other paths that fill out a life; they are aware of the traditional norms expected in each field, and they know they must follow them if they want to advance.

Each sub-culture has styles of dress, pecking orders of authority or reverence, even particular jargon. When that southern boy from Georgia moves to Boston and lacks the local broad Hahvahd, pahk the cahh (park the car) accent, you can bet he has to overcome some drawling y'alls and heah (for here) and I do declah (declare) to integrate sooner into his new environs. I have met many Americans who move to England for a year or more and return with a British accent. Perfectly understandable. They want to fit in, so they learn to pronounce words differently, like paytent for patent and shejule for schedule.

I remember being shocked to attend college in Pittsburgh and discovering that I had grown up in Miami Beach with a New York accent acquired from all the northerners around me. I was saying dawg (dog) and whawter (water) and awwfull (awful) as if I'd grown up in Brooklyn. I dropped it as soon as I realized what I sounded like and how much more softly others pronounced their words. I didn't want to be thought a New Yorker, especially when I was from Miami Beach.

We all want to fit in to become more accepted, gain admission and be one of the inner circle. It quenches our thirst to belong, comforts us and offers special privileges, opportunities, more intimacy, respect and certainly money. Who wouldn't want that?

There is nothing wrong with conforming to your work environment. Glance at the ballet students and dancers and notice how many women have their hair tight and bunned-up, the way it 'should' be. Watch soldiers managing their gig line that aligns their belt buckle edge with their vertical shirt line and their fly seam.

Every group has its rules. Sometimes it's clothing, which

is a major way that people size up a stranger. Some don't approve discussing money and how much you have. Others have no hesitation asking how much rent you pay or how much your house costs. Some don't approve of speaking loudly, especially in restaurants. Others can be so noisy at public dinners that I've had to ask them to tone down. There are hostesses who only permit impersonal chit chat at dinner parties. Sports is fine. Politics is taboo. I once heard about two, weekday, suit-wearing, country-home weekenders punching each other uncontrollably after a spirited discussion about political values spun out of control.

How bold are you to ignore these expectations when you want to be liked and included next time? The TV series *Billions* shows that after her billionaire husband's immoral actions become public, the villain's wife is stunned and hurt to learn that her child is not invited to another child's party. She uses her financial power to get even or get what she wants.

Money buys all kinds of entrée, of course. You can review the boards of countless prestigious museums and other non-profits and find the names sometimes of greedy, corporate raiders and other not-so-savory characters. It's all so calculating on both sides. But money paves the way for that kind of power and acceptance.

I remember decades ago being in the New York Metropolitan Museum's, Egyptian Temple of Dendur for a Philip Morris reception and being repulsed by all the people fawning at the feet of the company's President, George Weissman. I only saw a seller of cancer sticks, but my colleagues were schmoozing their client, who spent millions of dollars sponsoring art projects

Not surprisingly, George seemed to have trouble understanding the view of those who argued that arts organizations should refuse tobacco money as tainted. "Do you stop the Bolshoi from coming here because you don't believe in the Russian system?" he said in an interview with *The Times* in 1987.

After he retired in 1984, he became vice chairman of Lincoln Center for the Performing Arts and then served as its chairman from 1986 to 1994. His rise from son of immigrants to such power and prestige is an astonishing success story.

As I have been implying, if you want to move along your career path, you will have to decide how much you are willing to compromise. I took assignments from Philip Morris to build up my resume, so who was I to be so harshly judgmental.

There is the problem. It's so conflicting. I had started a photo consulting operation and was retained to hire photographers in different parts of the country to take portraits of successful women who were to be given awards in a Phillip Morris sponsored program. It was a great chance for me to make a mark with the many accounts in the large PR agency I worked in. I wouldn't help sell cigarettes directly, but I was willing to hire photographers to make the company look good.

Did I sell my soul? Not totally. I was certainly compromising my values. I am simply pragmatic. I have known other people who say they are too principled to make any concessions. Yet I think it's impossible to interact successfully with other humans and not compromise. Pick your poison. But financial survival and social acceptance were always high on my list. And one might always recall that when you work for someone else, that boss is paying you to do what he or she wants. Or the company wants. It's not your show alone.

If you want to assimilate into another group, you have to change yourself somewhat. For starters, how can my way be the only way? I am a very tolerant person. I can easily accept that others are raised differently. It was also obvious in my late teens that others had manners and etiquette that I didn't know about, hadn't been taught. I've mentioned noticing regional and foreign speaking accents. Once I left home, I also saw that I didn't know proper ways to eat at a more formal table: which fork or spoon for what dish and when, bread plate on the left or the right? How do you hold a glass of red wine, and why it's different for white wine and brandy. What can't you talk about in a formal setting? I needed to learn about tipping, gift giving, phone calling, behavior at work, subjects that were taboo, correct grammar. My upbringing omitted much of that.

If I wanted to be accepted—and I did—I had better learn what is expected. I studied two books about polite society by Emily Post and Amy Vanderbilt. I not only learned how to interact with others who had better 'breeding,' I saw that many of them didn't know some of the rules. Of course, I rarely told them even when they haughtily impressed others (but not me) with their insistence that a red wine should be refrigerated before serving (rather than at room temperature). Knowing the rules of etiquette gave me confidence and allowed me to be more relaxed with people of all social classes and backgrounds.

I remember laughing when one of the books described how to eat a mango: only in the bathtub. Because it's too messy a fruit to eat at the table. But I'd grown up picking them off my tree in Florida and taught many a northerner the polite way to enjoy them in front of others without embarrassment.

I encountered a delightful description about the benefits of good manners taken from a 2008 New York Times book review by Dinitia Smith explaining the keys to Emily Post's popularity: "Such books had always been popular in America: the country's exotic mix of immigrants and newly rich were eager to fit in with the establishment. Men had to be taught not to blow their noses into their hands or to spit tobacco onto ladies' backs."

One great benefit of learning all these traditions and expectations is that you can easily decide how they fit on you or if you can wear them comfortably. If you can't envision it, that's probably not the career for you. When I see politicians and corporate executives in dark blue suits, white shirts and boring striped, slightly-angled ties, I am horrified at the thought of wearing those garments every day. In my financial public relations job at Ruder & Finn (R&F), I wore three-piece suits, and I was often criticized for wearing ties that were too wide or pictured flowers. They wanted me to conform completely.

I like a bit of color and individuality. When I ran the Nikon Camera photo gallery, I had one sport jacket that was salmon-pink colored and another that was straw-yellow. But when I was fired from that job and looking for another, I finally realized that I wanted to wear jeans and sneakers every day, just like the photographers I loved hanging with.

Management at R&F, which was one of the largest PR companies in those days, knew that the younger execs were struggling with the business culture. They were smart to pay for periodic lunches, when we "Young Turks" could meet and talk about our problems and frustrations. It was very cathartic, and helped us blow off steam. We could console each other, bond, adapt and adjust. This was years before corporations were offered ropes courses.

I still remember a woman named Chris announcing one afternoon that she was glad to hear that other people had the same disenchantments and grievances that she had. She thought that she was the only one, and that there was something wrong with her. If everyone had similar complaints and dissatisfactions, it must be the job and the place. Not her. So she quit.

What a gift to learn in your late 20s that a culture is not for you. Move on. Find something else. That is what changing your life path or reinventing yourself is all about.

You are looking for the right fit. You spend 8-10 hours (plus commuting time) every weekday doing a job or career work that occupies you, earns money to satisfy some of those basic Maslow needs, and ideally excites and stimulates you. Don't accept being bored, watching the clock, living for the evenings and weekends. Especially when you are young and don't yet have the adult responsibilities of spouse, child and house. You can't give up so early.

What pursuits appeal to you? What do you like to do and think about? Who would you like to have in your daily universe? Which groups of people seem attractive to you? These are really big confronts if you want to love your career from the beginning or reinvent yourself later on. If you love it, you will work hard and be passionate about it. As your bosses and customers notice your enthusiasm, success and more money are more likely.

When I discovered photography at age 29, I felt that professional photographers were like a family. I wanted to earn their admiration. I wanted to stand out. I didn't want to be just another great photographer or an employed picture editor. I only knew that I liked looking at photographs and being around the people who made them. They were artists, but pragmatists. They had vision and knew about mechanical gadgets, how to talk to people, organize global shoots. The photojournalists were like soldiers of fortune, jet setting around the world, documenting kings and presidents and CEO's one day and homeless alcoholics or jailed criminals or beauty queens the next. The landscape specialists searched through the dinginess of the world and brought back images of beauty, spirituality and transcendence. The stories they told kept me enraptured for hours.

It took me six years of searching—while I still had a day job hiring photographers for corporate assignments, running the Nikon gallery and helping Nikon sell its cameras through my public relations efforts—until I figured out how else I could earn a living that meshed with my interests. Of course, I never gave up. I just repositioned myself as a publisher of promotional books that would help photographers obtain assignments. Later I did the same for commercial illustrators.

I was 35 when I started my publishing enterprise, as photographer Dennis Stock so pointedly corrected me. You do not have a publishing company, he said. "You and I are going to be friends for a lot of years. So let's not bullshit each other!"

But most of the world wasn't so nitpicky, and American Showcase was a big success. I owned it for 27 years until selling out in 2004. Our staff grew to 30 at its height, plus independent contractors. I was my own boss. One of my 'gimmicks' was telling the truth. People weren't used to that and liked it.

I am a frank guy. You can surely tell by now. Are you? Are you willing to speak your mind? Remember that in Japan the nail that is tallest gets knocked back down, but in America the squeaky wheel gets the grease. Let's find out where you fit in.

Did you know that there are only 1000 US corporations that have more than 10,000 employees? 17,000 with more than 500, 90,000 with 100-499, 500,000 with 20-99, 600,000 with 10-19, one million with five to nine. The 3.8 million with 1-4 are mostly mom and pop shops owned by people who are building a life, not a business. The total is just six million businesses[10] in America. All this per Jim Clifton, the Chairman and CEO of Gallup.

There are lots of cultural norms in those biggest 1000 firms. Suppose you are in one of them, with 10,000 or 100,000 others, all competing to move up that virtual ladder to at least a vice-presidency wage, a cushy office, company car and pension. You go to some important planning meeting, and you are wearing your dark suit and predictable tie or safe pearls, and your boss who grades you and can promote you and give you bonuses says something you think is outright mistaken or that you disagree with. Or maybe it's another worker like you who makes a suggestion that you think is awful. What do you do? Right there in front of all the others?

Nothing? Don't want to embarrass the guy? Don't want him or her to lose face? How about privately? Are you willing to speak up and make your point in the most diplomatic way possible?

In other words, are you willing to have a 'courageous conversation'? In this instance or even a less confrontational situation in which you don't 'go along to get along'? If you never speak up, you will never stand out. If you take the risk, it might be a black mark in your review column.

Feeling queasy? Not too comfortable with this minor test? Think that your good work will offset your rocking the boat? You should decide where you stand and fit as quickly as possible. What you need to do is find the right culture in which you can earn a living, enjoy doing it, being part of the team, working with others.

Maybe it's rare to be given major responsibility in those big corporate environments. Or too draining to spend time weighing words in countless meetings. Or you can't stand the need to be diplomatic and political all the time. Totally the opposite from working in a five-person shop, where everyone must carry his/her weight and your opinion is asked many times a day.

I can promise you that one great way to advance is to work harder and longer than everyone else. There are plenty of white-collar office workers ready to call it quits at five. I've worked on a time clock, where the bosses could see when I came and left. My friends have worked for state and city governments, where work practically ceased 45 minutes before the day's official end at 4:30.

When I was employed at Ruder & Finn, I would arrive at 9:30

(the official start time), work 12 hours sometimes, go home and eat and work more hours after dinner. My mother heard about it and was very concerned. "I work to live," she pointed out, "not live to work." She was right. I was married and had an infant at that time. It was too much. But I had lots of responsibility and was respected by my bosses.

When I said that I loved taking pictures of my child and wanted to do something with photography, the president of the company said that he had always wanted to have a photography consulting department and gave me the chance to build it, as long as I continued to carry out my normal responsibilities. And I did. I even went to David Finn's home many Saturdays, so he could teach me how to develop film and print black and white photographs in his darkroom. He became my mentor.

One very useful strategy in larger companies is to find a mentor, and if that person is advancing in the firm, you can glide along your path in that person's slip stream. If that person is already at or near the top, he will promote you much faster. Soon after George Weissman joined Benjamin Sonnenberg's public relations firm, he was devoted full time to the Philip Morris account. He was then hired in 1952 as assistant to the president of Philip Morris. In 1960, just eight years later, Weissman had catapulted to chief executive of Philip Morris International. Six years later, George was President of the company. From assistant to the president to his replacement in only 14 years. Astonishing. Clearly he was talented. But working for the president probably helped him immeasurably to rise that quickly to the top of the pyramid.

Sonnenberg, by the way, is credited with helping create, and even regarded as the father of, the modern public relations industry. I met him once, when I had been given my notice in the early 70s and was looking for a job. He met me in his house and office, which was at fancy 19 Gramercy Park on the East side of Manhattan. It was two town houses of 18,000 square feet and 37 rooms that had been combined into an American palace. It was once considered to be "unquestionably the greatest house remaining in private hands in New York."

"When we moved in, it was not all that grand," said his daughter, Helen Tucker. "Then as Father got richer and richer and reinvented himself as an Edwardian gentleman, the house got grander and grander."

Sonnenberg is a rags to riches success story. A review by Dan Carlinsky[11] about the book of Ben's life by Isadore Barmash, said the following: "Here is a poor boy from Russia who as a young man adopts the Edwardian look— Chesterfield, bowler, spats, cane and swirling mustache. He scrutinizes important men in New York and in European capitals, noting how they dress, speak and move, and takes here a trait, there a quirk as his own. But this neo-dandy is no mere colorful character. He is also a first-class manipulator."

He looked like an Edwardian gentleman the one time I saw him. I think I remember mutton chops, but can't now find any picture or reference to them. But I recall lots of face hair and a purple satin bathrobe, more probably a smoking jacket. He didn't hire me, but gave fantastic advice that I never forgot: "Son, you need some buckram up your behind!" It was hat stiffener, he explained. I learned later that it's heavy cloth impregnated with starch that dries real hard. Basically, he was telling me I needed a kick in the ass. I wasn't driven enough.

You see these paneled walls, he said to me. I couldn't afford them when I bought them. And that made me work a lot harder to pay for them. Now figure out what you want and go get it.

Those walls, I read recently, were "in the second-floor drawing room, which was called the William and Mary room after being paneled with 17th century oak from Streatlam Castle in England. Sonnenberg, a renowned art collector, decorated the walls with paintings from Goya, Seurat, Cezanne, and Renoir."

Ben bought his palace from railroad tycoon Stuyvesant Fish, whose wife Mamie,[12] "was a commanding presence and prominent socialite of her day."

Sonnenberg continued the socialite tradition of the home. Astors, Rockefellers, and Vanderbilts partied in the fifth-floor ballroom that was 25 X 40 feet. Writers John Steinbeck and Langston Hughes attended his parties, as well as actors Henry Fonda and Lauren Bacall. The guest list of one party in 1967 included Bob Dylan, Jackie Kennedy, and Truman Capote. Sonnenberg is quoted as saying every party should include one actress, one businessman, one artist, and one banker. Ben died in 1978.

Exclusive parties always interest me as events that stroke the egos of those invited. Has anyone ever told you that they didn't want to go to a party, but they are upset if they are not invited? Even the most famous and accomplished people still choose to go to some special affairs. To be seen, to be comfortable with their peers, just to be with their own kind, or to be with talents who can stimulate them, appreciate them, maybe dazzle them too. Often such frequent congregations of notables became informal clubs, where the regulars are welcome and can relax with fellow affluent and distinguished people.

Spend a lot of time thinking about which groups you like to hang out with or want to have as your social and professional peers. Many politicians are elected partly, because they project an image that they would be great guys to have a drink with and that they are very accessible.

Do you want to part of the neighborhood bar scene, the country club or private social club crowd? Maybe the political action committee, volunteer firemen? The sooner you see which group is for you, the easier it will be to advance in your career and your life.

CHAPTER SIX

CHECKING YOUR ATTITUDE

You have probably heard a million times that you should "change your attitude." Especially when it is negative, when you are somber, in a funk, not fun to be around, or too serious. But it's almost impossible for most people to do anything about how they view the world, particularly if hurtful or damaging childhood experiences make you wary, suspicious, untrusting or defensive. Obviously, your attitude affects how you are perceived, and that is a great influence on how much career and financial success you will have.

I often heard I was: "too serious," and a business associate was always telling me to: "lighten up." He was so annoying that one day, when he had terrible setbacks and was facing possible bankruptcy, I am ashamed to say I needled him by asking: "Why don't you just cheer up?" Of course, he growled at me, and did not appreciate or take my advice, nor could he cheer up as his economic dreams were disappearing.

I was very miserable in my mid-thirties, after separating, then divorcing, losing my little nest egg in the stock market and having limited career prospects. But a few years later, I had a successful company of my own, was traveling around the globe for business on the expense account, had women friends and was feeling happy and accomplished and affluent.

I often ask myself: "How the hell did I get to this magical place? What made the difference? Why me?" The answer I kept coming to was that I had a positive attitude. It allowed me to see my situations in altered and beneficial ways. It helped me deal with difficulties with optimism, rather than a mean or defeatist defense. It often worked seeming miracles.

When I grew up, my father was president of the Miami

Beach Optimists Club. He was one of the happiest people I ever met. The back of his business card said: Keep Smiling. He danced into his mid-80s, and he was a very likable and decent human being. He was a great role model.

My mother was quite the opposite, having been so poor that her family of seven watered the milk to make it stretch further and would all share one small chicken for dinner. She grew up with hand-me-down clothing, never finished high school as a child, lacked textbooks she couldn't afford and was smuggled into the States from Canada, though she was eventually smuggled back to Canada and entered legally and became a US citizen.

But all those early experiences made her fearful, afraid of life, and of being noticed and feeling worthy. When my parents went out dancing, he wanted to be first on the floor, before it became crowded, and she wanted to be last, so no one would see how poorly she danced. Amazing they ever married and stayed together for 25 years.

The huge difference in their attitudes about life and people should make anyone choose to be casual, relaxed and easygoing like my dad. But it just isn't that easy. My own childhood setbacks and failures took their toll. Growing up without a father around, because he was away in the Coast Guard during the Second World War, probably made me anxious and more worried than those who had two parents at home, more money and better family time.

Yet, I changed. Somehow. I now know from experience that it is possible. Maybe it can happen to you too. Now don't think I am always upbeat or in a positive mood. Just most of the time or I can change my mood.

Let me give you an actual example of what happened to me one day. I was playing tennis with someone better than I am and wanted to show him how much I had improved, since the last time we played six months ago. I had been practicing my serve almost daily, either in games or alone. Of course, the self-imposed pressure was too much, and I failed miserably, my team lost many games when I served, and I was dismayed. I drove home feeling sorry for myself, that all the practice hadn't done a damn bit of good, and that I certainly hadn't impressed my friend.

I have no patience for any wallowing in this kind of self-pity. I know that not one person in the world should have any sympathy for this 'failure,' however disappointed I was. I knew I would gradually snap out of my downcast mood.

Within five minutes of being home, my wife told me that a friend, aged 65, was sick and had been given just two months to live. How is that for a kick in the face? For him, not for me. Here was a reminder of how rough life can be. Serious setbacks are what millions of people face every day: job loss, sickness, insufficient funds notices. How hard is it to keep my life in perspective? Well not very difficult at all. Just being able to play tennis at all at my age is a gift, so I have no right to let a bad game bring me down in the slightest. Learning to think like that 40 years ago is what helped me see my life more clearly.

I read a lot of books in my 20s and 30s about metaphysics and Asian/Far Eastern ways of thinking. I liked Zen Buddhist attitudes, and Alan Watts had penned a very graspable intro to Zen called *The Book* that I read was intended for his children. When my publishing staff used to whine about how hard our competition was, I paraphrased parts of *The*

Book to help them deal with our difficulties: there has to be evil to contrast with good; there can't be foreground without background; there can't be white without black.

Sometimes they'd groan about my "unsympathetic mumbo jumbo." And sometimes it helped them deal with the reality of life and living in it more gracefully. It has certainly aided me in dealing with obstacles and failures. I have never lost faith in one's ability to overcome or work around or completely bypass our burdens.

Studying the Japanese martial art aikido for three years was of enormous value. I often said that its principles helped me succeed in business and become rich. What I learned on the mat was easily transferable to daily life. This was no meditating in a cave away from society. This was how to deal with the attacks from all places in everyday interactions.

If someone tries to hit you, or verbally abuse you, you can obviously fight back with a block or counterattack of your own. He shouts, you shout. He hits, you hit back. He curses, you curse.

But aikido teaches you to pivot 180 degrees, so that you are side by side with your opponent, who is still swinging where you were, and off balance with momentum. A simple downward tug on his arm will propel him so far forward that he will be unable to stand and will fall to the ground, at which point you can sit on him or use an arm hold to immobilize him.

When my customers complained that my printer had screwed up and ruined their promotional advertisement, I did not say they were wrong, I was right, they didn't know what they were talking about, and that I was going to do nothing. That would have been a verbal block or counterattack. Instead, I surprised them by often agreeing with them, apologizing, and asking how I could make it better for them. More often than not, they would say, "Well maybe it wasn't that bad after all. How about if you give me a discount in the future or a small immediate credit now?" More than half of the time, I would say yes.

Flowing like this makes life like a ship on gentle waters. There is an ease in living, a success in dealing with people that is more like sunshine and breezes than storms and dark clouds.

It's the exact opposite of what happened to a friend of mine, when someone called him a schmuck behind his back. My friend was determined to get even, and he would carry the hurt with him until he had revenge. He was not going to let her get away with such a nasty comment. "It's not right," he rationalized, when I told him that life is short, ignore the negative stuff, and urged him to forget about it. Of course, I agree that his critic was out of line, but my friend probably carried this grudge around for days, until he had some kind of satisfaction.

Look I'm no saint. It took me months to go up to some guy who told others that he didn't like my tennis style and excluded me from his doubles games. I didn't mind retelling the story I heard of how I was ostracized by this strong player, because I did lobs and drop shots that he hated not being able to get to. I thought it was laughable.

I finally felt ashamed, and went up to my critic and told him what I'd heard, that I enjoyed playing against his much harder and challenging game, and that I understood why he'd prefer to not be frustrated by my style that one friend who taught it to me calls 'junk ball.' He appreciated my candor, conveyed his point of view more precisely. I told him I understood, and we parted with more mutual respect. Not only did we end up playing in games again, but he even gave me advice and a free tennis lesson.

I hope it's clear that this kind of attitude works wonders in business situations as well as all other aspects of your life. It's invaluable when connecting with others. It also will help you when your problem has nothing to do with people, when you are struggling to achieve a financial goal, reach a higher athletic plateau, hesitating to choose a new career.

I did not acquire this attitude instantly. It took years of practice and trial and error. It came to me especially by my not forgetting how terrible things could really be. Did you lose some money in a business deal? Why not rationalize with yourself, and keep those setbacks in context? Believe me those losses will pale in importance if you learn the next day that you have only six months to live.

In fact, I used to take vacations with my kids and pretend that I did have just six months to live. I often wondered if my staff thought I had no right taking a long weekend or an extra day or two at Thanksgiving or Christmas with my kids. But we only have one chance to live our lives, and I worked very hard to get those extra days off. I would think about a friend who found out he was dying and wondered if he thought about the days he didn't take to be with his family.

You see all of us have problems and situations that are damnable and difficult. It's how we interpret them and deal with them that matters. You have heard that they are "opportunities for growth." But that is not what you want to hear, when you think your life has seemingly ended or taken a horrible turn for the worse.

I can rationalize all the time. Three women I dated are dead now. It saddens me that they are gone, even though I hadn't spoken to some for years before they died. But death keeps things in perspective. How can I get upset over cold string beans in a restaurant? I might ask the waitress to heat them up, but I am not going to freak out about it or become grumpy. They are only string beans.

I think you already know how life usually 'works.' It's not fair. My mother taught me that, when I was two years old. Other people have benefits they didn't earn, just inherited. Others have taller, prettier, stronger bodies. Some have smarter brains. Some win the lottery. You have to deal with what you have. Make the most of that. Ralph Waldo Emerson said that each person is superior to you in at least one way. That works from your point of view too: you are superior to each person you meet in at least one way. Discover what it is. Capitalize on it. Savor it.

Learn about attitudes in other civilizations and integrate some of them into your daily life. In much Chinese painting, the humans are smaller than the mountains, because nature is dominant. That is a way of viewing the world and your life that is quite different from Western Renaissance art that shows large human beings with a small storm and lightning way in the background.

Do you see yourself as one of those large people in a Western painting? Are you self-centered, know you are very important and think everything and everyone should revolve around you? That might have worked when you were an infant or a small child. However, as an adult, you may find that you are frustrated, people interactions aren't so satisfying, and a lot of times you come across as an insensitive jerk. Consider changing who you are. You will be happier, if you ever notice there is a difference. But if you are reading these words, we both know that you are open to change. That's a healthy first step.

Here's an easy exercise you can work on every year: when it's your birthday. For decades on my special celebration, well-meaning friends and relatives have been needling me. You too, I bet. On reaching 30, I couldn't be trusted. In my 40s I was middle-aged. After I turned 50, I was an old man. Then came grandpa teasing. It has been a continuous barrage of jovial taunts and insinuations with a smile that I was entering a less desirable period, no matter the actual number.

But about 25 years ago, I realized that a girl I was close to in high school had died at 17. So had a cousin and a niece died as teens. Women I dated passed in their 40s and so did lots more friends after 50. I began to see how unbelievably fortunate I was to still be alive and that each birthday, each larger number was a glorious gift that I wanted to savor and appreciate. Each past year was full of fantastic moments, emotions, some adventures and satisfactions. Sure I wasn't as fast or strong, athletic or balanced as in younger years. But just being alive is such a blessing.

Now it's so easy to cast off or dodge those verbal assaults that comment on how old I am. The higher the number, the happier I am. I hope I reach triple digits. Can you also adopt this attitude about aging? 'Possibility Thinking' is another whole area to explore. Many people shut off options in their life by saying something cannot be done, a path should not be taken, a dream should not be pursued. That will kill your progress or any change.

Why not do your best to say, "What if..." instead. "Maybe I could change my circumstances, find a partner, make more money, relocate, improve my quality of life." So start making the slightest effort to change something, no matter how small. If no one is there to kick you in the butt, to get you off the line you are frozen on, you have to do it yourself.

The first time I ever jumped out of a military plane, I was the first man in the door, waiting to reach the drop zone from 1250 feet up, the wind almost blowing me out, and my eyes on the red light in the front. When it turned green, the jumpmaster gave me no time to think about it: he punched me hard in the ass, and I was flying into space without a thought or fear until I realized what was happening.

In our everyday civilian lives, there is NO jumpmaster. We must take the leaps ourselves. Yes, it will be scary. We are all afraid in the beginning.

Most of us can learn to overcome those anxieties and become relaxed with feeling uncomfortable. Just take small steps, go for tiny changes, don't be hard on yourself, if you don't transform yourself overnight.

Discover who you are, learn what your pace is for taking on new projects or behaviors, and ignore others who tell you to move faster or differently. After all, it's your life, and you are the only person who understands deeply what you are truly about and what you want.

On the other hand, a psychiatrist told me that if your early life subjected you to hurts, failures, parental abuse or abandonment, poverty, setbacks, disappointments, then you are likely to be a teenager or adult with a poor attitude and a not-so-positive view of how the world works. "That's a bad break," she acknowledged. You are justified to conclude that you are infused with bad luck and grew up in crappy circumstances. Even if you are a rich kid, a beautiful girl, a well-built physical human, you can still have a mental filter that sees living as a terrible, frustrating and doomed experience.

Her conclusion is that it is very hard to change your attitude. Your circuits are wired in ways that result from your early interactions. But it is possible to change how you perceive your life. It takes a great deal of work. In her opinion it takes therapy, a willingness to discover what some of those early disasters were, accept that you are not to blame for the raw deals that happened to or by you, and to move on out of that deep hole of depression or sadness through introspection and the guidance of a therapist.

I have never been in therapy. But I had two girlfriends who saw their shrinks two to three times a week. Coincidentally, both were extremely bright and had photographic memories. Neither could understand why I couldn't remember the name of a restaurant we went to six months earlier, while they could repeat the exact words of conversations we had during our dinner there.

I was humbled. But I was also happier. Four years after I broke up with one woman, she sabotaged her career and ended up in a mental institution. She eventually committed suicide, as had her sister who jumped off the Golden Gate bridge. Perhaps, there was just a sad set of genes in those women's DNA. Perhaps, no amount of therapy could have ever helped them. So I am not suggesting that all you have to do is make an attempt. Sometimes there are forces beyond our control that won't let us change our attitude without intervention.

It is intensely difficult to overcome years of unsatisfactory conditioning on how to survive financially and emotionally in the jungle that we live in. But I am sure that it is possible. As the psychiatrist promised, if someone is seeing a therapist, that client is usually open to change. That is the first and best step in making that change.

A Catholic priest made a similar observation. He told me that if a murderer comes to confession and tells him that he plans a mass killing, the priest is not allowed by his vows to run to the police and warn them about the planned mass killing. But the very fact that the killer has come to confession is, the priest believes, a signal that he wants help and would welcome a cup of coffee or walk in the park in the hope that his church Father can talk him out of the plan he knows is wrong.

You don't have to believe you can change. You only have to think that it may be possible for you to change. A million kids grow up in poverty, and a few, like Colin Powell, rise up and become successful-he rose as high as Chairman of the Joint Chiefs of Staff, the highest military rank in the United States. Maybe he had a mentor, a loving parent, a teacher who urged and coaxed him on with her support. Perhaps you can be one of those few who rise like a bird out of low and crappy beginnings. Why not make a tiny bit of effort to find out? The fact that you are reading these words should convince you that you are different or somewhat special, because only a tiny fraction of readers will ever bump into these thoughts.

You have a chance, you have an interest, you have a curiosity, a restlessness to change something about yourself. You should welcome this opportunity.

CHAPTER SEVEN

EARNING RESPECT TO REACH YOUR GOALS

*"Other men are lenses through which
we read our own minds."*
RALPH WALDO EMERSON

How far would you go to earn or retain the respect of your cohorts? Would you kill a stranger, your child, yourself? People do that. Can you believe it?

I mentioned Maslow's hierarchy of needs earlier. After physical survival and safety, financial security and love, people then want not only to belong, but to have the respect of the members in their groups. It may include a higher status, public recognition, fame, and prestige.

Do you want to be famous or at least acknowledged as someone special among and by your peers? Probably. If not, I am sure you at least want to be admired and respected.

Many people gratify these ambitions with their hobbies, rather than in their professions or businesses or trades. They show the pony that's awarded blue ribbons, they win cooking contests, grow the largest pumpkins, know more sports statistics. They love the applause, the cheers, the acknowledgement, the certificates of merit. They feel accomplished and special with these achievements. As they should.

I think it's great that people enjoy these non-financial pursuits and satisfactions. I mentioned Emerson's words about how, "...every man I meet is my superior in some way, and in that I learn from him." So, if you are open and humble enough and interested in other people, you can tease out, be stimulated by and enjoy everyone's area of specialness or expertise. However I don't see people acting like that. Instead human nature wants us to be the one who is respected and listened to. Some also want to rise and be at the top of the pack. Mamie Fish, whose husband sold Ben Sonnennberg his Grammercy Park palace, "...was determined to unseat Mrs. William Walter Astor as the grande dame of her time." There are people at all social and economic levels who want to first belong, earn the respect of their group, and then prove themselves superior, to be acknowledged as more famous. It is that basic animal need that I have referred to. Never forgetting this drive by many to be the top critter will help you maneuver in the business coliseum and many other arenas.

A gang in the slums may be no different in some ways for its members than a high society club is for its elites: a place to unwind, enjoy your bro's, hang out together. But then the gang might want you to romp together, steal together and maybe rape and kill together. I never belonged to a gang, but I have to believe there is some truth to the documentaries, movie scenes and written descriptions I have encountered. There may be an initiation ritual. There might also be moments, when a member has to perform an illegal act that forces him to cross his own line of what's right or wrong.

To win or retain the respect we all want so desperately, the vile deed gets done. The drug deal, carjacking, handbag theft, convenience store robbery. There might be a shootout and wounded losers. When some die, someone did the killing. Can you imagine pulling the trigger, just to stay in the gang and have a home away from home? To risk prison, if not your own death? Impossible for me to know.

The groups most of us join are not nearly so threatening. But then most of us in the States grow up with parents, a bed, a home. Not all of us. I have trained in the very deadly, Brazilian martial art, capoeira, with illegal street peddlers who ran from the cops, and other capoeiristas who thought they might have killed people in a fight. I was one of the few white guys, certainly an alien in a foreign world just a few blocks from my Manhattan office. Our mestre named me Gringo. I studied for three years, enjoying the acrobatic moves, the fellowship, and the music that accompanies this dancelike form of aggression and survival. We even went together to Bahia and Rio in Brazil, took sweaty lessons in meager classrooms and watched local capoeiristas entertain tourists in upscale night clubs. How far would you go to earn respect?

If you were drafted for military service, and the enemy was approaching your buddies—who come to mean everything to you—you'd kill, and it wouldn't be illegal. It's what you are trained for, your mission. Not killing to save your friends would be the source of your shame and loss of respect. Context is everything. I am certain that no one can ever know what these moments are like without living them. Movies and novels only convey the slightest idea of what that is really like. One night as the Officer of the Guard in Korea, I had to enter the dark building that housed trucks and road graders to find the thief who had cut through the chain link fence that enclosed our remote compound. I had loaded a round in my .45 caliber pistol. I was 22-years-old and scared out of my mind. Not a romantic, glorious second to be had, and I never found the thief. Although at another time one was shot running out of the compound with a stolen meat slicer. I had already heard from older sergeants who had been there during the war about how horrible war and killing and the sadness were. I have no illusions about it.

I spent 13 months in Korea living in close quarters with about 20 other officers. I wanted to get along, be respected. It was a challenge from the start, because I had earned my commission through a college ROTC program (Reserve Officer Training Corps). West Point career officers had higher status. I did get some points for having become a paratrooper. But just a few.

I was always someone who didn't like following all the rules. So, in the army, away from family and normal social interaction, I was more outspoken than many about the army in general, and its rules and conditions. I complained about the frogs in our shoes, the lack of women to date, the crappy living conditions, and military life in general. The headboard of my bed had a bullet hole in it and the mattress was blood stained from a West Point graduate who felt his career was ruined when the battalion failed a test he oversaw. So he shot himself.

I made the best of my time in the military. I had a decent attitude even then. I learned to speak a bit of Korean, had friends in Seoul I could see every month or so on leave. I enjoyed Korean food, was the liaison to the biggest orphanage in Korea and located Christmas-present money for the kids among other things. I met people (especially nurses) at the hospital a mile away and arranged for some Koreans who needed surgery to be admitted for treatment—it was good practice for the staff. Another career officer just one rank higher than mine was miserable and hated that I was enjoying the tour so much more than he was. His envy and disgust finally came to a head at dinner one night. We were all sitting at a table when this man picked up his vanilla ice cream with his fingers and smooshed it all over my face. It was a good lesson about jealousy and dealing with others.

I can't emphasize enough how hard it is to understand other people, until you put yourself in their shoes, even if they are your age and from a similar background. It's almost impossible if they are from another culture, whether a different region of your country, another continent or even a distant neighborhood in a large city. Humans are messy and complicated. It's important to keep an open mind, to not assume that your values are universal and reasonable and make sense, especially if you are an outsider or newcomer who wants to join an unfamiliar group.

What do you feel about honor killings? Where families kill their children, because they believe they have brought shame to the other members. This is a crazy notion to American culture. Killing our children for not agreeing to an arranged marriage, being a rape victim, or dressing in unacceptable ways. It's primarily females who are stoned, stabbed, beheaded, beaten, burned, strangled, shot. The poor girl might have wanted a divorce from an abusive husband or had an affair.

No matter the reason, a family or tribe or clan feels it has the right to—and has to—protect its honor and respect in the larger community by killing the daughter who even just appears to have brought shame. The BBC suggests maybe 20,000 a year are killed worldwide. And not only in the Middle East and Asia. In 2010, there were almost 3000 honor crimes of violence (not killings) in the United Kingdom.

This seems unbelievably severe to us, but we come from a different culture. Much more forgiving and tolerant. I mention these extreme examples of group norms to soften your angst and annoyance, when you encounter a group you think you want to join for financial or social benefits...and discover you are questioning some of its customs and practices. At that point, maybe earning and retaining the respect of its members isn't so important. That's a huge realization. Think again about what you are doing.

Review your long-term goals. Ask yourself if this path is one you want to follow? If you do care what these people think of you? And if it is right for you, and you still do want to be a respected member, then you should adjust willingly, accept the compromises, and enjoy the ride, having learned more about who you are now in your growth.

If you are uncomfortable, can't accept some of the prejudices or preferences or what seem like ridiculous stupidities, don't care if you are respected or honored or elected club president, then you better move away as soon as possible. Even if it means choosing another career or lifestyle or place to live. It takes more courage than you imagine. You may bemoan all the effort you put into being invited to join and doing what it took to achieve some status or specialness. But it's time to move on.

In large cities, you have myriad possibilities and groups to mingle with. There are all kinds of people and jobs, ideas and events, places to visit and shop and discover new art and culture. You find variety and sophistication, liberals and conservatives. And the more people you meet, the more likely you will encounter some who can be helpful in your business and financial pursuits.

Much of monetary success originates with knowing others who have unusual ideas and patterns to share. Who might offer you opportunities to work with them or make money, because you both have common values in whatever non-business activity brought you together in the first place. It's one of the reasons I left Miami Beach and made my way in New York City. You can also be anonymous, so that if you make mistakes, not everyone will know about them.

It's much harder in small towns and rural areas. There is less freedom to be who you are without the gossip and judgments that are common in a tiny universe. There will always be those with power they acquired after years of maneuvering or by inheritance. Winning their respect and access to their clubs might be a huge uphill journey. The eccentric and different and uncommon thinkers are not always welcome or included. I know this too, after living 25 years in villages of 1400 to 4000 people, where many still think I am a newcomer, compared to their families being entrenched for generations.

Among the benefits that impress me in my little town is how someone could move here and join a church group and become more integrated in two years than I was in 15. Connecting through volunteerism is common, whether being a member of the fire department, a charity, or the historical commission. Many people donate hours and hours of their time. Maybe that appeals to you. Maybe it's easier. Maybe you can make a name for yourself more readily. You can give to the group in any way that suits you. As you spend more time and become more of a contributor, your esteem will rise in the eyes of its members.

My friend Peter is a retired lawyer who spends hours making objects in his woodworking shop. He built benches for a local bird sanctuary for quiet watching. He also carved and painted wooden models of birds that could be sold by the non-profit to raise money. These were labors of love, and I heard first-hand from the head of the organization how respected and appreciated his efforts were.

I have been involved with land and preservation trusts, the historical society, the organization that helps boys with no homes or parents or who have broken the law and were awarded a chance to learn a trade, rather than go to jail. However, I am not a natural joiner. It's just not in me to seek those activities as eagerly as others. You have to figure out what works for you, what and who you really care about. Which groups of folks you'd like to interact with. Then you will participate passionately and with enthusiasm. You will be good at helping realize the goals of the group and its members. You will earn their respect with your contributions.

Living in big and small communities was perfect for me at different times in my life. In both cases I figured out how to make money from an office in a skyscraper and then a desk in a farmhouse. The fax machine and later the internet have been glorious gifts for those who want a life with mostly trees instead of concrete. A young woman in Tokyo told me that New York City is like a graduate school for life. But then I burned out of city life and spent over a decade figuring out how I could survive in the country. You just have to be willing to change and adapt and reinvent and relocate and discover which places and groups are important to you, and then how big a cheese you want to grow into.

One last clique to mention is the warrior class of feudal Japan known as Samurai. These men were so devoted to their warlord and a code of honor that they were willing to kill themselves at the mere command of their leader. If they had disgraced themselves or shamed their fellows in any way, they would sometimes request the noble, ritual suicide called seppuku or hara kiri instead of a more conventional execution. Sometimes the warlord himself would commit seppuku as part of a peace agreement. The public ceremony first requires self-disembowelment with a short sword, and then another samurai severs the spinal cord at the neck with a larger sword. Try again to imagine a society so devoted to its practices and traditions that its members want to die by their own hand if they violate the rules they have all agreed to. Their honor, and the group's honor, and especially the leader of this band of brothers must be followed and respected at all costs. This code, called Bushido, The Way of the Warrior, was formalized in later centuries, before the samurai disappeared in the late 1800s with the arrival of western culture and the ascendance of the mercantile class.

You probably wouldn't have wanted to join that group if you'd had the chance. Becoming a chivalrous, European knight in shining armor may have also been a little too much. You can now see how easy it is to make some choices about what you like, where you can see yourself, with whom you want to belong, or if you want to be famous or acclaimed in a much larger milieu, like a national or international stage.

We all want to belong, somewhere, somehow. We need peer respect. If you are not sure what you want to do to make more money or change your career, where you want to live, then why not work backwards and identify groups you want to affiliate with? Maybe then you can figure out how to reinvent yourself. Just remember that you will have to earn people's respect. You will have to make people feel comfortable. You will have to embrace or at least accept other people's values and customs. Can you do it? You have probably already done it many times. Look back and see when it felt right or good or pleasurable. When were you happy? Was it being a member of a high school sports team that won the championship? Maybe you can isolate some part of your unique and varied past and use it to build a new career. Good hunting.

CHAPTER EIGHT

DEVELOPING
DISCIPLINE

If one strategy for achieving your goals—especially those involving career, money, and success—is to never give up or to keep practicing your skills, then the next logical question is: What do you do if you don't have the discipline to make yourself keep trying and practicing? It is easy to know you should stop smoking, make another cold sales call, knock on another door, send out another resume, etc. However, not everyone has that temperament.

I didn't used to think of myself as a disciplined person. And I am still not in many areas. One friend always has his taxes done by April 15th. I usually squeak by the last week or two before October 15th, after two extensions. I am often late to meetings; something always comes up. I can't make myself go shopping for new clothes until they start to get faded with loose threads.

Forget about polishing my car or buying the latest computer. For years, I was still using my daughter's hand-me-down Blackberry, rather than the iPhone the rest of the family has.

On the other hand, I can accept my disinterest and resistance to activities that are very important to others. And I have acquired techniques to deal with areas that I do value, despite my lack of discipline.

Exercise is one good example. I always knew it was important, but I never could make myself do it.

Friends had regularly scheduled Tuesday evening tennis games or weekend softball leagues. Not me. My life was so chaotic and demanding that it seemed impossible to commit myself like that. After all, I either worked so hard for others when I was an employee, or so hard for myself when I had my own business, that it was unthinkable to also cram in a regularly scheduled anything.

Aha! One solution was to have a dumbbell in the office. Now I just had to remember to pick it up and strain my biceps. Surely I could do that once a day. Ha! Not a chance. Years went by, and I never picked it up. It even became invisible; I no longer saw it sitting there. Thank goodness it wasn't a dog craving petting.

In 2007, four years after I had sold my publishing company, I joined a gym for the first time. With more time available, I made myself go once or twice a week. But it was uphill all the way, because the drive to the gym alone took over an hour round-trip. After two years, I admitted defeat, disgusted with my lack of discipline and uninspired by the gym rats there four times a week or friends who had been going for decades at least two to three times a week.

I told myself I could do five minutes a day of anything at home. No driving, no locker room dressing. It would be easy. But it never happened, until one day I'd had it with my mental slovenliness and challenged myself to perform. Something stirred inside of me that shouted at my laziness. Eventually, I began to do push-ups, abs crunches, some barbell moves, the only pressure I kept on myself was to do at least five minutes a day.

All this in addition to whatever tennis playing I did, because I had started that in 2007 as well. Tennis was fun. Exercise was a chore. Within a short time, I had strung a few days in a row, then weeks, then months. Of course I told my friends and family what I was doing, partly for support, but mainly for pressure. I wanted every edge to force myself to keep on doing it. Just five minutes a day. Sometimes I did as much as 20. Whatever I could do. The consecutive days kept piling up.

Later I read a Lifehacker article by Gina Trapani about upcoming comedian Brad Isaac, describing his conversation with Jerry Seinfeld,[13] who said he wrote jokes every single day.

He (Jerry) said for each day that I do my task of writing, I get to put a big red X over that day (on his wall calendar). "After a few days you'll have a chain. Just keep at it and the chain will grow longer every day. You'll like seeing that chain, especially when you get a few weeks under your belt. Your only job next is to not break the chain."

"Don't break the chain,"[14] he said again for emphasis.

"Don't break the chain." Sounds easy enough. But it isn't. One of the reasons I could do the daily exercise is because I had practiced being disciplined in some other ways. I read years ago that it's good to finish a hot shower with cold water to close your pores. I tried it. It's not too bad, because your skin is already hot. But you certainly notice the slightly shocking difference. I always do that.

Before I finish the hot part of my shower, when my legs and back are warm, I lean against the wall and stretch both legs. Then I slowly bend over. Some times my longest fingertips can touch the floor without bending my knees. In younger days, all five fingers could, and on rare occasions, my knuckles. Finally, I do the healthy-shock, wake-me-up-in-the-morning cold-water thing.

You'd think that I could stretch my legs during my daily exercise. That a simple touching of my fingers to my toes would be easy to attempt. But that isn't for me. I developed an alternative strategy. Whatever works. Figure it out for you.

By the end of May 2020, I had gone 3,125 consecutive days of at least five minutes of exercise. I've also taken some scorn for getting out of bed at midnight or exercising at 1:30 am, when I'd forgotten on a vacation or had a late night out. I had to do my exercises. No matter what. Even in a one-man tent in Mongolia.

This daily exercise has messed up my meal schedule too, because I can't eat until I've done my required drill. If I do eat with everyone else, I have to wait until the food is digested. My life is big-time changed. It is a regular habit in my everyday routine, and it has helped me be disciplined in other ways.

One area that I've always had some discipline in is with food. When my older girls were under 10, one of them told me my breath smelled bad, and she didn't want to kiss me. Oh, my goodness! Bless her innocent, devastating candor. That was horrible. How to deal with that one?

I decided that it might be the digesting meat in my system that was causing the smell. Rotting flesh, I told people. I'd also heard that it takes eight pounds of grain to make one pound of meat in a cow. I was doing a good deed for the world's hungry by eating less grain, indirectly. But could I give up my love for rare hamburgers, lamb chops, steak tartare?

Being able to kiss a daughter without seeing her recoil was a big motivator. It worked. The smell of my breath did change. My daughter stopped avoiding me. Plus, I stopped feeling so tired and sluggish after each meat meal. I was a different person.

I had to remember to tell people about my eating habits. I was okay with fish and fowl. But I can still remember a friend inviting just me to his apartment, and I refused to eat the high-priced, delicious-looking steak he'd bought and cooked for the two of us. Awkward.

Just for laughs, I must tell you about my daughter bringing for the first time a young man she'd been dating to our Thanksgiving dinner in the country. I proudly offered four dishes of wild game I'd shot myself: doves from Argentina; turkey, pheasant, and squirrel from Connecticut. Her date was the purest kind of vegetarian. He was unbelievably strict and disciplined. He would taste none of the delicacies. It was just vegetables and dessert for him. Awkward.

I gave up red meat, veal, and pork over 30 years ago. Occasionally, I taste something, like chorizo sausage on a trip to Spain. Even, a lamb specialty that was the only main course served at a celebratory dinner one time. Everyone always says, "Oh eat it, what's the big deal!" They don't get it. They are not disciplined, and they sometimes suffer for it.

In 2005, I suddenly learned that my cholesterol had shot up to 239. I didn't even know what cholesterol was or which foods had it. I was eating ice cream every night, sometimes, two healthy full-fat yogurts a day, bisques and cream sauces galore, and all kinds of cheeses. I didn't know an HDL from an LDL (was that like an LOL?), but I did discover right away that 240 was heart attack range. I was in trouble.

Some people just pop a statin pill and keep on eating whatever they want. But, I had taken less than 10 aspirins in my adult life at that point. I guess I am a bit of a purist, when it comes to meds and drugs. I went cold turkey. Right to zero fat yogurt, olive oil instead of delicious butter. Goodbye to manchego and brie cheese, and sorbet replaced ice cream. Soy and almond milk replaced 2% regular milk. I wasn't fooling around here. These were life and death issues, I believed. I wanted to both live a long life, but also a healthy and fit one.

Again I encountered feedback from friends and family that was not supportive. "You're overreacting," I heard. I realized they didn't like that I might be judging them and their own lack of discipline. It was a rough time for all of us.

Nevertheless, I love food, but I love good health and long life more. I am not willing to accept "5-10 less years of living" in exchange for the pleasures of all the foods that are "too good to give up." In this area, I can be disciplined. I don't know why. I don't really care. I just see that these actions I can do. The challenge, like simple daily exercise, is to develop alternatives to the areas in which you can't be disciplined.

For example, I've always wanted to write a book. Non-fiction, not a novel. Had my pen name picked out in elementary school. Actually, I wanted to be a writer, but after years of fantasizing, I discovered I really didn't like writing. I still loved books, and even became a publisher. However, spending all those hours sitting by myself instead of interacting with the world and talking to friends was never a choice that was real for me.

I noticed that I wrote long letters to family and friends over the years. I also kept journals in my 20s that stacked up to a foot high. But writing was no way to make a living, until I discovered public relations. Then I could feel the joy of crafting words, and it didn't matter to me, whether I was writing a speech or a caption. I was happy forming phrases, regardless of how commercial and meaningless they were.

Decades later, I still hadn't started my book. Didn't even have an idea for one. I did start a blog about health and fitness in March 2009. I wrote an average of once every two days (850 posts over 1800 days) and I kept it going. Just barely. I didn't care to spend time pushing for viewers. Once again, I was just practicing a skill and disciplining myself in a tangential way. Almost five years later, I finally started drafting this manuscript.

Nike says, "Just do it." The phrase originated from convicted criminal, Gary Gilmore, who said "Let's do it," just before he was to be executed by a firing squad. Gary had no choice. But we do. Making any moves towards a goal can be the hardest steps in the world. I am a very practiced procrastinator. Are you? Years ago, I told my friend Joe, "Just take one little step in front of another. Don't worry about how you are going get across the whole street."

We all do things in our own ways. Hopefully, some lead to success and satisfaction and result in more money, recognition, and maybe even fame.

As I write, I have no idea if this book will be published and have an audience. But by having a glimmer of a dream and having some semblance of stick-to-it-iveness, and some writing achievements from the discipline of a blog, I am as ready as I'll ever be to give it a shot.

CHAPTER NINE

THINKING OUTSIDE THE BOX BY DARING TO BE DIFFERENT

In 1960, at age 19, I saw the Paul Newman movie called *From the Terrace* that showed the path to money and success.

There is a scene where Paul's character drives down a Connecticut country road in the winter and sees a small boy ice skating on a pond that suddenly breaks open. The boy falls through the ice and Paul rescues him. The boy's grandfather is the country's most famous financier and is impressed with Paul's courage. In gratitude for the rescue, Mr. Moneybags hires Paul to work at his firm. Paul performs brilliantly, rises through the ranks, becomes partner, and very wealthy.

For years, I told people that all you needed to do to be successful was drive around Connecticut in the winter and keep a lookout for large estates with kids playing outside whom you can save when they fall through the ice. Yeah right! This could never happen in the real world.

Boy, was I wrong. And that is one certainty I want to describe. Life is filled with random events beyond your imagination and logic. If you are open to them, see them, and are willing to grab the opportunities that come your way, you will marvel at how easy it is to achieve your goals. You do need to have courage, some money, skills and patience. But in my long search for a satisfying career, I remember hearing that success is the intersection of opportunity and preparation.

Randomness is all over the place, even if it doesn't involve saving a rich man's grandchild. I know a young woman who just graduated college and was about to accept a job offer on a Monday. At a party the night before, she met a stranger who told her about a different job opening; she interviewed for that one on Tuesday and was hired on the spot. After I gave a speech, I shared a cab with someone I knew on the panel. A few paragraphs later, something clicked, and we started a business together that lasted over 14 years.

In college, my Panamanian roommate complained that I was showing friends what was wrong with their life choices, but not suggesting how to correct their errors. Like a tennis coach telling his students they were swinging the racquet wrong, but not telling them how to get into the right position. Back then I had an inkling of what was needed, but my solution was still incomplete.

Now I know that part of the answer–as I have already said–is practice, practice, practice. Practice makes perfect...if you are practicing perfectly.

In addition, I am now talking about changing your worldview and thinking and acting outside the box that others are functioning in. That is a very big challenge! It will take a lot of practice.

Because most people are unhappy...because most people are not rich... it's obvious that you don't want to do what most people do...otherwise the odds are that you will be unhappy and not rich.

When I was in second grade, my report card said, "Ira will defy authority, when he thinks it is wrong." I've always been proud of that teacher's note to my parents. That personality trait made it possible for me to defy the "appropriate" ways to live and make more money, and finally, out of frustration with failure, set out on a new road that worked magnificently.

A psychiatrist friend told me that less than half of the people alive (or maybe just in America) are reflective—think about their circumstances or imagine how they might change them. Most people don't think much, they are too busy living from day to day, paycheck to paycheck. If you have read this far, you are likely in the smaller, more thoughtful, and ambitious group. I know that each of us is different, formed early on by our genes and upbringing. But I am convinced we can change, without being forced to alter our lives by terrible traumatic experiences.

Let me begin this incredible and true adventure with some anecdotes.

However ridiculous or unimportant it sounds, I knew after wearing three-piece suits for business that I wanted to earn a living wearing jeans and sneakers. It seemed so easy, casual, and relaxed. Although it was certainly not for everyone.

When I met a suited, former colleague years later on Fifth Avenue in Manhattan with a watch fob in his vest and both hands up in the air, because his nails hadn't dried from his manicure, I knew that he had taken a path not for me. (I later read in the Wall Street Journal that he'd gone to jail for taking kickbacks from suppliers for recommending their services.)

I liked taking pictures of my children, so I decided I wanted photography in my daily life. I liked viewing picture books, so I inched into a career publishing them. It all seems so inevitable in retrospect. But it wasn't. I drove people crazy with my constant searching for a better life. Cost me a marriage and some friends who were sick of my not settling for 'normalcy.'

I never gave up. I merely ached for goals that suited me. I was often envious of that lucky minority who know since childhood what they want to do. You hear those stories all the time: "The first time I saw an actor on the stage, I knew…" "The first time I went to the ballet, I knew…" "I would collect rocks and use the microscope my dad gave me for a Christmas present, when I was seven…"

Not me. I was 35, before I figured some things out. I had no idea that I wouldn't be working for others and would have my own business. I hoped for years as I strained to define my goals that I was a late bloomer who would flower someday, before my rat-race life was over.

I was inspired by famous people who started new paths in their 30s. I learned that Nobel Prize-winner Dr. Albert Schweitzer hadn't given up his successful music career and begun studying medicine until he was 30, that the painter Paul Gauguin had been a stock broker and was a failed tarpaulin salesman at 36, and that the Pulitzer Prize-winning poet Wallace Stevens had been a lawyer and stayed an insurance executive until his death at age 75.

By the ancient age of 35, I had discovered enough about myself to be sure I was ready to take the big gamble—I was going to become a publisher.

I'd known for a long time that I was more of an inner-directed person who made decisions based on my preferences than an outer-directed person whose values and choices were often dictated by what society and one's peers thought was the way to live, act and dress. I had a head start in turning out as an outsider who wasn't part of the group.

When I was young, my father, a chiropractor, was called a quack, because doctors like him were thought to be fakes who knew nothing. Occasionally, I had fistfights or took verbal abuse about dad's profession. It was easy to become alienated. We were lower middle class. I had no car, couldn't buy new clothes often, much less from the fancy "in" shops and had to work after school, when others enjoyed sports and school activities.

I grew up in Miami Beach in the 50s (like the TV series *Magic City*), where there was one high school educating kids of all economic strata. One boy's father owned a third of the Empire State Building, another girl received a hotel as a gift for her 16th birthday. I visited a girl in my high school who was signing checks for $5000, before we hung out listening to music. She skied in Europe.

Others with much less—some almost poor—lived in South Beach long before it was renovated and fashionable. Just like in the movies, they had ducks-ass haircuts, cigarette packs rolled into their t-shirt sleeves, and were rough. I was invited to a birthday party of a 'South Beach girl' who was a classmate. I was in the living room, when someone threw an 8-inch knife into the coffee table there. I can still see it swaying left and right. All that birthday girl wanted was to get away from that life. She did. The girl grew up and achieved her dreams of owning a pink Cadillac and wore furs.

Being in the middle, sort of, I wasn't part of any group. I was busy surviving. When at age nine I asked my parents for a baseball glove, my mother asked me if I thought gloves grow on trees. I had a job the next day, delivering newspapers from my bicycle for $5 a week. I learned to sell subscriptions and collect the money from customers each week. Sometimes I was soaked delivering papers in torrential Florida rainstorms.

I once sold so many new subscriptions that I won a free trip to Cuba and received the key to Havana from Batista. Others from school went on trips around the country or the world and were handed gifts of money for just being alive. I may have envied them, but in the end, my need to work turned out well for me: it taught me discipline and responsibility. I also learned that it wasn't so bad being an outsider. It helped me to think differently than those in the group.

I graduated to being a cabana boy for $2 a day every day after school and on weekends. I met tourist girls, while handing out towels and sweeping up cigarette butts. It was fun, but it wasn't elegant. I learned to dance the cha-cha-cha to hang with the northern girls at night. Sometimes, on the beach, we "watched" the "submarine races" in the ocean. My little town was a world of strippers like Zorita who danced with a boa constrictor, Silver Dollar Jake throwing foil-wrapped condoms from his convertible, classmates with professional gamblers and mobsters in their families. It was different and special, and I was still not included. I had to make my own way.

I also learned two other unforgettable lessons at the hotels. One time I walked to the cabana manager to apply for a job, and he told me I was fired before I was hired, because I walked too slowly toward him. First impressions are very important.

Another manager, Murray Arshall, said, "You never know..." suggesting that things you do and say can come back to bite you. Your reputation can be everything. Guard it and nurture it like it's alive. People will judge you by what they know and hear about you. These days, the internet does lie, but your deeds follow you everywhere forever. You never know...

At the same time, I had so much fun growing up. My little league baseball 'career' was full of laughter. Pitchers are supposed to throw a fast and menacing ball if you're good. My weak pitches were so slow–but accurate– that power hitters would swing before the ball ever arrived. I messed up their timing. I once struck out 13 batters of the 18 minimum I faced in a six-inning game. Being different has its' advantages. Unfortunately, when I advanced to pony league at age 12, my pitches couldn't reach home plate, and that career ended forever.

One summer during college, I was a soda jerk on Lincoln Road, the main and chic shopping street. I admit I cut myself and bled once into a rushed cherry jubilee. I loved serving the Honeymooner's Delight created by the Austrian owner: a banana split that had the ice cream on the bottom, a covering of whipped cream, and then the banana lying down uncut on the top with two scoops of orange sherbet at one end, a cherry tooth-picked on the other end, and a line of whipped cream traveling down the banana from the cherry to the two balls. It was a giggle. The couples who ordered it always loved it. Plus, it taught me it was okay with some people to be crude, unconventional, outrageous, unexpected. You could succeed even with a banana split to make a buck and a lasting impression. Just make it different.

"Different" is good. Of course, I didn't know that when I was younger and being made fun of. Outliers like me are often lonely or disheartened or sad when they are left out or ostracized by others. It has its advantages: you learn by default to think 'outside the box.' It's a gift in disguise, but most of us don't know it. We feel sorry for ourselves and wish we could be "normal" and fit in with the others.

As the years passed, I realized that there were others like me who had different tastes and values from those I grew up with. I was fortunate to be accepted at a college (Carnegie Mellon in Pittsburgh) that had art and drama majors along with techies. Being eccentric or weird or unconventional was common there. It gave me confidence in being out of step with those in the traditional marching band of group thinkers. Seeing the world through different eyes gives you an enormous advantage over people who were raised to conform, be a team player, or not rock the boat or stand out in the crowd.

I already mentioned the raised Japanese nail that is hammered down first, and that the squeaky wheel in America is the one that gets the grease. But even in America, you are expected to conform.

What can you do if you are merely one of the mob? What if all your life you were taught not to be different or special or distinctive? That is the situation for most people. Can they change easily to even have unorthodox dreams, much less actions? How likely is it that if they even come up with a new vision, that they will have the courage and the stamina to go for their dream? To leave the pack and become a lone wolf? Start a business? Switch careers? Take a job in a different field? It's damn hard. Near impossible for many. I will discuss this challenge in the next chapter.

Back to those out of step. You have heard your whole life about famous successes who dropped out of school or defied their peers. They put up with, or resisted, the group taunts and authority figures who told them to stay in line and stop being a wise guy. Is that who you really want to be?

I remember my son at the age of eight, standing on the grass, on his first day of summer day camp, being told all the rules and who was in charge. At the end of a 20-minute lecture, the kids were asked if they had any questions? I am still bemused that he asked, "When was the universe created?" Everyone laughed, the counselors had to look serious and not even smile. But my boy was thinking differently, even then. Nevertheless, most people are straight and conventional. I think it is very hard or almost impossible for those tigers to change their stripes. Society must civilize its youngsters by teaching them to behave—sometimes for their own good...like around a hot stove—but primarily to obey laws (so people don't infringe or hurt others), develop social graces and polite interaction, be predictable enough to obtain employment, respect, advancement, etc. All to help you manage a life in the company of normal society.

Sounds well and good. But after reading about the innovations of the few stars who made millions, won applause, wrote bestselling books or earned Nobel prizes, how is the average person in his teens or 20s supposed to imagine that "little ol' me" can become a creative individual? If you are 10 or 30 years older than that, is it too late to act in any way other than your comfortable and familiar behavior?

Sir Ken Robinson[15] is an educator who writes and talks about how all kids are creative, but our schools destroy the creativity in most of us. Make us afraid to speak up or suggest offbeat ideas. His YouTube video, "Do Schools Kill Creativity?" is the most watched TED talk with over 18 million views. Most of us have rushed through that gauntlet in our youth. No wonder thinking innovatively is harder than it sounds.

A famous artist named Duane Michals, told me that people are like a huge cloud of semen all swimming for the egg. There is only one winner—the first sperm that reaches the prize. The millions of swimmers who were too slow are flushed down the toilet.

Also of all those people who are born and live, only a few, like Jesus, Mohammed, Einstein, and Beethoven, change the world. The rest are merely dross who grease the wheels that keep the species surviving. Most of us just aren't going to make big waves.

Now you and I know that even if you are not a Bill Gates or Nelson Mandela, you can still make some key difference in fewer people's lives. There are countless examples of those who help others in their countries or neighborhoods... volunteers and do-gooders who provide shelter, compassion, food, support. And there are spiritual-inspirational providers, be they pastors or painters, musicians or mentors. There is much we can do to make lives better for those around us. Or add some creative product or everyday service that will improve the comfort and joy of our fellows during their struggles on life's journey. Remember that there are six million businesses in America. Maybe you could own or be a major player in one of them. Dream about it!

That said, it is still a humongous challenge and effort to start viewing the world from a new perspective, when you have only practiced with the ordinary approach. When I was a kid, I ate sour cream and cottage cheese together. "How did you ever think of that," someone asked in amazement. I was amazed—shucks they are both on the same shelf in the refrigerator. How hard was it to make that?

On the other hand, I recall the first time someone told me he ate bananas with peanut butter. That startled me. Silly that I would react that way. But I did.

The biggest puzzle to me is this. I know that humans are social animals, and most people want to be part of the herd. They want to be included, whether it's the street gang or the country club. Nothing is better for many than being accepted by those you respect or feel kinship with. Even if some of that group's habits and values are distasteful. It's why kids smoke before they are teenagers. It's why dinner party racism or bigotry goes unchallenged. We all have a need to belong. Maybe it's the residue from earlier times, when you needed your fellows to protect you from predatory animals and conquering tribes.

But as a middle-class person, in the 21st century, there is a paid army to do the fighting. What I saw clearly as an outsider, as a youth who was rejected by the in-groups, was that many of the kids and the adults were not so happy. The parents' lives often seemed repetitious and dismal. I asked myself over and over: why follow the path that promised boredom or why jump into the rat race?

Thus, I turned out differently. I had less money. I had to work after school, from third to 12th grade and even during college. I came out into the postgraduate world with debts from college loans. I had to make something of myself or fail in the effort. I was determined, but confused. I initially had no mentors or guides.

I questioned everything. One photographer signed his book to me with the words, "May you find your answer."

When I saw Chorus Line Off Broadway and was exhilarated

by the music and lyrics and told a friend that I wanted to do something that was as entertaining or had such a good effect on people, my friend said: Can't you just enjoy it without thinking of yourself?

Painful. Disheartening. I often felt that I was making my path by bushwhacking in a dense jungle of vines with a dull machete, yet here I am now, where I am happy to be.

CHAPTER TEN

PRACTICING DIFFERENTNESS

What can you do to be different—to win the race, to be rich, successful, have a satisfying career and life? First you must realize that if you just do what others do you'll never stand out. I wrote my first resume on tan paper, not white, and I had three vertical columns of typed information, like a newspaper, rather than just one column seven inches wide, like a book or term paper. I was always looking to make a first impression that was different from everyone else's.

Chris Phoenix business card.

Years ago my son worked for a company that had a very creative business card: it looks like an airline boarding pass:

But life is far more complex than a resume page or a business card. I started being an outsider long before being an outsider was the cool thing to do. Now, so many young people think 'outside the box' that innovation and creativity is almost the norm and expected.

If this isn't you, then I suggest you start priming that behavior pump. You must do some uncomfortable things, like wear two different colored socks sometimes (not on a job interview of course), or less predictable clothes. Take a different route home, don't drink as much as everyone else, don't date only those you are expected to be seen with and whom others think are "appropriate" for you.

Experiment with novelty. Take some chances: read some books that aren't on the best seller lists, sign up for an unusual class. I know people who took tango lessons and then trips to Argentina to practice their dancing skills. You could study hand drums, yoga, an exotic foreign language, not simply Spanish or French, maybe it's Japanese or an African dialect. Go visit some of those confronting and totally unfamiliar cultures, either by heading overseas (if you can afford) or attending local lectures and museums. Put yourself in situations where you are shaken up and forced to see the world differently than how you grew up and have lived so far. You don't have to go out drinking with your buddies after work every night. Make some new friends your old friends wouldn't guess you have.

I believe I read that Van Gogh made a big breakthrough, when he could squeeze yellow on his palette. You need to have some new colors and behaviors in your life too, if you are going to start thinking and acting differently from those around you.

There are loads of books and articles with ideas on 'How to Become More Creative.' Many of these are simple, like "play with clay." Some are very deep, like the 752-page book by Arthur Koestler I read decades ago titled, *The Act of Creation*. A friend who advises corporations on how to rethink their bad, suffocating, or losing practices told me about the field of Possibility Thinking. Explore these.

Most important is your willingness to change. You must be motivated, be okay when your friends confront you, and believe there is a benefit, a life-changing one. Watch the movie *Working Girl* about a secretary from Staten Island who wants to advance up the corporate ladder in Wall Street to become an executive doing mergers and acquisitions. Her successful struggle always makes me tear up, something I rarely do. But all her friends– even her boyfriend–don't want her to rock their boat of traditional patterns. Too confronting.

You should have heard the friends' warnings when my wife and I left Manhattan to live on a farm. They said that we'd be miserable, that there were not any good restaurants, no culture, no bright people, our kids were going to have no one to play with. However, we wanted a rural, natural, animal-filled experience. Those "friends" from the city felt that we were rejecting their chosen lifestyle. Many of those supposed friendships ended. They were either envious, resentful, disillusioned, or thought we were crazy and no longer worthy of their time.

But now I have peacocks and exotic pheasants in my life, rather than just city pigeons. In fact, I have a flock of beautiful white pigeons. Of course, it's not for everyone, but I had to find out if it was for me. It still is after 30 years.

Back to practicing differentness. From the 'Become More Creative' Google search, I read at Entrepreneur.com[16] that: "Fifty five percent of employed U.S. adults would leave their traditional jobs to be self-employed if they could be sure of their financial stability," according to a recent study. That's over 83 million people.

What do these individuals want that their current jobs aren't offering them? Apparently, creativity: 36 percent of employed adults want to quit their current jobs to pursue a more creative position. They're even ready to sacrifice their paychecks, with 29 percent saying they would be willing to take a pay cut for a job that allowed them to be more creative.

That is a huge part of the working population that is dissatisfied. Jobs are not common these days. New employment is hard to find. Your current job might be a dead end, but are you willing to attempt a change? You must be the individual who thinks differently than all the other stuck employees competing with you for jobs or new businesses searching for customers.

The silly part of the statement above is, "if they could be sure of their financial stability." No business or job comes with that promise. That is like saying you want to give birth to babies without any pain or sail on a boat if there are no waves. The two are incompatible. They don't go together.

So, if you're serious about making a change, whether it's in a job, relationship, place to live in, life style, whatever, you have to be willing to take risks. Change is very uncomfortable. You already know that from hundreds of previous life experiences.

However, I'm skeptical that advice like doodling, writing in the bathtub, (during a bath, like Beethoven) or painting naked in the bath water like Salvador Dali will do the trick. But don't care what I think. Try anything anyway. Just take one action that is a break in your normal patterns. A first step. Then another. And another. It takes practice.

I saw a video about people who do dance walking on Fifth Ave in New York City while listening to their favorite music.

They look silly, none are in suits or elegant. But they are happy and smiling.

You need to shake up those brain circuits that tell you how you are supposed to act. However, those circuits can also be your friends. Ask them what you like to do? And what you know about already.

If you are a working stiff selling manual labor, like the boyfriend of Melanie Griffith's character in *Working Girl*, the odds are against your becoming a rocket scientist or brain surgeon. But even that boyfriend saved enough money to borrow from a bank, buy a boat, and become a lobsterman. That was his dream, and he made it a reality.

In his book *Zig Zag*, research psychologist, Keith Sawyer, proposes various steps to becoming more creative. One puzzles me: "Ask the right question." How the hell are you supposed to do that if you are someone who isn't naturally creative and sees things differently? But it's like the challenge I mentioned earlier of identifying the correct problem, before working on a solution.

I often refer to a chapter in *Megatrends*, which described all the railroad companies going out of business in the 20th century. However, one chief executive redefined his company as being in the transportation industry, not just the railroad business. That firm survived all the railroad company bankruptcies around it.

Sawyer's advice (emphasized in italics that follow) is to become more original by *practicing every day* with simple problems as well as some specific exercises.

You must *become an expert* in an area before you can be creative in it.

Listen to TED talks. They're free videos of inspiring, funny, or fascinating speeches made by brilliant people. To get started, check out 6 TED Talks Every Entrepreneur Should Watch.[17] If the videos don't load, google "TED talks" and search that site by the speaker's name.

My wife and I went to the first five TED (Technology, Entertainment, Design) conferences. They introduced us to CD-ROMs, and we heard Bill Gates, Steve Jobs, the president of Adobe (created Photoshop), the guy who invented hyperlinks, saw the first public presentation of computer voices, saw the first car GPS system, was one of the first 3000 people to experience virtual reality, etc. Clearly, I was interested in these subjects. That is why I returned to the conferences. You can see thousands of these talks on YouTube. Scroll through and watch some that catch your interest.

Find a mentor. Almost all successful people are willing to pass on their experience to worthy newcomers. That is why they teach or work for non-profits or turn to philanthropy. Just seek someone whom you respect and might respect you. I used to attend speeches and then ask questions of the speaker afterward. I made some friends and acquaintances that way. I certainly wasn't going to meet creative, accomplished people in my early measly job environments.

You can also *imagine who you want to be*. Picture the revised you five years from the start of a new adventure. Then take those small steps, one after another, to get there.

Become a beginner. Take up a new activity, like archery or juggling. Don't be afraid to make mistakes and fail.

Just keep practicing. I did this years ago when I went to an after-school program for kids to learn juggling (along with the town's mayor, we were the two oldies) from world famous juggler/motion-artist, Michael Moschen. You should have seen me wowing my adult children and grandkids at our group's performance in front of 500 people. I also took up archery to hunt turkeys over a decade ago. Much more difficult and sporting than the shotgun I used to harvest a bird twice a year. I only reaped two toms in a dozen years with a bow. And this was long before I ever heard of The Hunger Games.

Koestler's *Act of Creation* Links Humor (HA HA), Art (AHHHH) and Science (AH HA) by claiming all three utilize somewhat related brain patterns. They bring two seemingly different and unrelated elements (he calls them matrices) together in an original third way.

The jokes and funny stories take you down a road that should lead to a predictable result, but suddenly arrives at an unexpected conclusion. The destination is a safe startle out of nowhere, a bit of a bait and switch, and we release our emotional tension and surprise with laughter.

Artistic insights often connect unrelated elements into a blended, new and satisfying way, although the two initial elements might still be recognizable. A pointillist makes a painting from tiny pixels of paint that reveal the whole from a distance. The cubists show a side view and a front view of a face in the same portrait of the head. In art, we accept illusion vicariously (it's only paint, they are only actors reciting lines). We experience the emotional mood and spirituality that the artist felt or intended.

The scientist has the satisfying conclusion of resolving confusing observations by rearranging different facts: if the earth rotates around the sun, rather than the sun traveling around the earth, then our observations make sense. Eureka! Of course, sometimes those pronouncements can get you killed by the people in power who call you a heretic or mad man.

Per Koestler in *The Act of Creation*: "the principal mark of genius is not perfection but originality" (p. 402). He argues that, while the emotional context changes, the psychological processes that supported the generation of original results is ultimately the same in humor, science and art and involves the bisociation of previously unrelated matrices of thought. The importance of creative thought, and Koestler's ultimate motivation in studying it, is eloquently described:

"Habits... reduce man to the status of a conditioned automaton. The creative act, by connecting previously unrelated dimensions of experience, enables him to attain a higher level of mental evolution. It is an act of liberation—the defeat of habit by originality" (p. 96).

Koestler affirms that all creatures have the capacity for creative activity, frequently suppressed by the automatic routines of thought and behavior that dominate their lives.

Thus, we can free ourselves from habit with originality, and we can practice being original by starting with differentness. It's difficult, but it is possible. It takes willpower and practice. But where does one begin? Maybe by laughing or thinking about what makes something funny. Maybe by mixing paint into pictures or going to museums and looking at breakthrough painters or art movements.

Maybe by reading about scientists who had revolutionary insights.

Do you want to do it? Are you okay with a tiny bit of change? You may need to leave friends behind or some familiar habits and routines in the past. Can you picture the benefits and new satisfactions? Excitement? Accomplishment? Contributions to yourself and others? It may be there just for the taking. Try it. You will probably love it.

Don't forget this thought by a famous entrepreneur and venture capitalist who co-founded Netscape and many others:

Marc Andreessen ✓
@pmarca

⚡ Follow

9/Since we are social animals, the challenge of actually standing outside of herd is brutally hard. Pressure to conform is constant/intense.

2:12 PM - 7 May 2014

CHAPTER ELEVEN

SPOTTING TRENDS

Over 30 years ago, around 1987, I returned to Pittsburgh for a Carnegie Mellon University reunion. I graduated in 1962, so a lot had happened since those memorable days. One conversation I never forgot was with the taxi driver who brought me from the airport to the campus. I mentioned nostalgically that the sky used to be pink from the glow of steel mills and pouring slag. He confessed that he had worked in those mills and was just earning money temporarily as a cabby until the plant reopened. I guessed it had been 5-10 years, since that mill had shut down there. Yet this poor guy was still hoping.

Globalization wasn't a common word then, but relocating factories to emerging countries with cheap labor was well underway, as was the manufacture of cheaper steel by Japan, South Korea, and some countries in Europe. In the late 80s, I also met a brilliant economist who was writing academic papers about these relocations. She warned me that it was going to totally alter the American and world economies.

If only someone had told that cab driver what this ginormous trend was about, he might have thought more about a different job or career. He didn't spot the trend.

In 1984, I began going to the first five TED conferences, where brilliant achievers (like Steve Jobs and Bill Gates) in the fields of Technology, Entertainment and Design shared their stories about the present and the future. I even suggested to TED's founder, Richard Saul Wurman, whom I knew, that we should create a book together called *Trends* that would give readers a heads up about major changes coming in the broad society. It would allow people to change their careers by preparing for new jobs or the end of old jobs. It would describe social trends foreseen, as well as changes created by new technology and other forces.

The book never materialized, but I was aware of, and noticing, trends ever after. They changed my life, and I tried to change with them. Whether as an employee or as an entrepreneur. I am not talking about predictions for 100 or 1000 years into the future. I am talking about trends happening five years or so before and after now.

If you can recognize a trend, you can be a step ahead of everyone else who doesn't. If a field or industry is growing, that is one you might want to get into as a worker, entrepreneur or investor. If the trend is going in the opposite way and diminishing, then it's obvious you should avoid entering it...and if you are currently in that shrinking part of the economy: get the hell out, before you are fired or bankrupt.

For example, long before email, there was this new thing called a fax machine. It speeded up communications and allowed my publishing business to prosper. You didn't have to wait days for a letter to arrive or have the extra expense of overnight delivery. Yet, when I eventually bought a house and was communicating with the builder about renovations, he didn't fax and continued to drive 20 minutes each way to give me a contract or to sign a change order. Cost him an hour he didn't need to spend. The fax was too new-fangled for him to buy one and figure out how to use it. So he remained inefficient and less productive.

The end of the Soviet Union was in the wind after 70 years of a failed communist experiment. You could certainly guess that things were changing. But who knew what to do about it or how to accelerate it? I could never have predicted just when it would all come apart, but the book I helped publish about the USSR became possible during those years of change I hoped would be happening. And after the Citizen Diplomats like myself were done with our early activities, other people and companies swooped in to start new businesses—or work for them—and make billions of dollars. It was good to speak Russian then. Have you heard that it might be useful to speak Chinese?

I knew of retouchers who made $300,000 a year doctoring photographic film for ad agencies. After Photoshop was available, they were out of business, as were some still photographers who had been asked for years to take another picture with a different color in the background. There were many assignment shooters who used to earn tens of thousands flying overseas with models to have an exotic background in the shot. After Photoshop, there was no need to send them; clients would just use the computer to merge an existing (stock) photo of that Hawaiian sunset and beach with a New York studio shot of the person with the product. Slews of those photographers disappeared as well.

Trends resulting from technology changes are the easiest to spot: CD-ROMs, internet, cell phones, color TV, video streaming that is nibbling at movie theater ticket sales and closing video stores. The list is long.

Social trends aren't so difficult to identify either: women's lib, Fox News and TV cable channels, Tea Party and gerrymandering, gay rights fights. Have you heard that 70% of Americans are now overweight or obese? Won't that affect the food industry, the health services, insurance costs, taxes?

Recognize any effects already in the economy? How about climate change, water shortages and droughts, alternative energy from sun and wind, fracking, outsourcing, online retailing like Amazon-what is that doing to retail stores and shopping centers? Uber and Airbnb. Global warming and pollution—what is that doing to the coal industry in America?

When a friend wanted to enter the newspaper field, I informed him about the losses and shutdowns happening there. When a hopeful young photographer asks my advice about making a career in print journalism, I tell them about the increased competition from amateur cell phone pictures and fewer outlets.

Of course, some people still enter these shrinking areas, and some of them will earn a living. So will some struggling actors and singers who stand out and have super talent. But the odds are more against you in a declining field than an expanding one. At least learn which direction your field is heading.

We all need to be looking for trends. Especially these days, when the people in power are deceiving us every minute. The corporations don't tell us that the food is bad for us. The politicians promise us anything to win our votes. The media will advertise almost any product or service that pays the fee. And most people will be fooled by advertisements. That or they won't even notice what is happening and how it is currently affecting them until it's too late. But you don't have to be taken. You can avoid being naïve and gullible. You can be one of the few who sniffs the danger in your surroundings. Whose mental antenna are out and aware. Who is anticipating how things are likely to change, so that you can take big steps ahead of the pack "just in case" your sense of caution is correct.

Of course, you may have to change jobs or relocate to another city or state. You may even have to train yourself for a new field, while you still have an income from the industry you are in that is going down the tubes. You may have to give up some of those nights drinking with your pals. You may have to put up with their mocking and teasing while they tell you how silly you are. But it will be worth it. You will have a better chance to land on your feet than your buddies who didn't see the trend or didn't worry about it when they saw it or didn't take steps for the next phase of their lives. You will have the last laugh after the plant closes or the store where they worked lets them go, and you are ready for, or already working in, a new job situation.

Want to see a trend? Coal mining production in the United States. Here are the number of employees, both above and below ground, in various years: 784,000 (1920), 488,000 (1950), 193,000 (1975), 131,000 (1990), 80,000 (2013)

So, if you are a miner, you might do whatever you can to find a new career. I don't want to be flippant about it and suggest that it's easy to make this change. It's probably almost impossible if you are born into a mining family and there is little money, hardly any free time, no way to retrain, etc. I get it.

In the movie, *October Sky*, based on the book *The Rocket Boys*, four high school students in a coal mining town use their free hours to learn how to make rockets in the face of all the scorn from their parents, classmates and others. One teacher was a mentor who inspired them, and the author's mother was also supportive.

Homer Hickham, Jr.. wrote this inspiring, growing-up story of how he and his buddies won a National Science Fair gold medal and scholarships to college. After that, Homer worked as an engineer, including 17 years at NASA, where he trained astronauts and managed some aspects of the Space Shuttle and the International Space Station. He has written 17 books, and *The Rocket Boys* won many awards and was #1 on the *New York Times* bestseller list. The other boys who built rockets with him also got out of Coalwood, West Virginia, went to college and had impressive careers as businessmen, banker, engineers and entrepreneurs.

This is a helluva story. It's rare enough to be made into a movie. These kids were driven by science and rockets and encouraged to go for their dream.

They could never have had a dream as big and wonderful as their lives turned out. After they left town, the mine closed. They knew they wanted to be anything but underground miners. So they took chances and worked hard at it. And when those rockets they built stopped blowing up and eventually zoomed into the sky, their confidence grew, and they suspected maybe they could achieve other goals.

Can you see any trends? Do you have any dreams, no matter how insane they seem? Do you have any skills that might be special? Or at least competent, capable? Can you write them down? Are you willing to risk rejection and failure? Those are big questions. But if your answers are

"Yes" to most of them, you should refine how you might change your life. Or at least modify it and pivot a bit.

Tad Floridis told me we are living in a "dynamic society, things will change, globalization and the internet in the last 20 years have eliminated many jobs. You better adapt."

"Even when I was a publisher, and the book business was booming," Tad explained, "I did not present myself as only a publisher. I saw that IT (information technology) was up and coming, and I learned about it, got involved with start-ups in the software-as-a-service space. That was how I positioned myself. I was who I was becoming, not just who I was." And he did pivot to being involved heavily for a while with software-as-a-service and e-books.

This relocation of manufacturing overseas is disastrous. The factory shuts down, then the employees are out of work. Next many of the small businesses that were making a living partly from the plant workers lose revenue, struggle, often have to close. It's a vicious downtrend.

I don't believe the politicians one bit who promise that they will somehow convince Congress to change laws that will change corporate policies and strategies to bring those factories and jobs back. You should not trust them either. It will take years for the few businesses that come back. Sometimes the labor costs for one hour of an American factory worker's time can buy a whole day of a laborer in an emerging country. You can't compete with that!

For the most part, we are now a service economy and not a manufacturing society. I get angry when I hear politicians promise to bring back factories or to revive the coal industry and increase the number of coal mining jobs just to win votes. Most people may not see through the nonsense, but just look at the numbers above. Coal mining is a dying business. You should be on guard. To protect yourself from political leaders who are trying to mislead you. Do whatever it takes to get out of shrinking fields while you can.

In April 2016, Peabody Energy filed for bankruptcy. Founded in 1883, it is now the largest private-sector coal company in the world. It joins four other large coal companies that have sought bankruptcy during the recent slump—a result of tougher environmental policies, a flood of cheap natural gas and a global glut of metallurgical coal that's dragged prices for the steelmaking component to the lowest in more than 10 years.

Along with dying industries and globalization reducing jobs, there are technological advances that will create new industries and increase hiring opportunities. That is terrific. You should identify them and decide if they appeal to you. Maybe you'd like to be part of them. How about the burgeoning outer space industry? Did you know that there are companies currently developing mining equipment for asteroids? Sounds like something out of a sci-fi movie, but it's already happening. You should always remember, however, that corporate management is determined to use as few employees as they can. Have you seen how Tesla can build a car in a factory using robots? With a minimum of people. Check out this Wired video on YouTube.[18]

This is the future, and it is here now. Think twice about betting your career on those manufacturing line jobs, even in growing industries.

Did you ever wonder how fruit and vegetables travel from the field to your supermarket? How about the role mechanization has played in changing the game in that industry? In 1960 California, there were 45,000 workers harvesting tomatoes. Ten years later there were less than 5000, and most of them were riding the machines that had been developed to do the picking. The tomatoes had been re-engineered to ripen uniformly at the same time, so only one pass through the fields was necessary. The water content was also reduced and the shape of the tomato was redesigned to be oblong to reduce cracking when it was transported in bulk.

This will be the future. The present is now. Trends like these are unstoppable. You need to notice them and see when— not if—they will affect your industry.

Of course, I am not supposing that you are picking vegetables or mining coal. I am only making the point that automation, mechanization, computerization, climate change, etc., etc. are happening. They are trends that might affect you now, shortly or in the not-too-distant future. You have to pay attention, before you are out of work, and you must plan for this onslaught while you have time to develop new skills.

Think about finding another way to earn money. You should put effort into redesigning yourself. Maybe you need to become a self-starter, maybe even become entrepreneurial. You may have to change where you and your family live. But please don't wait until it's too late and you just received the dreaded pink slip announcing, "You're fired."

Do not think that you are safe if you have a high school or

a college or even a graduate school degree. It just isn't so. Haven't you heard about all the white-collar employees who are laid off? Or that 45% of new college grads are living at home? What about how many kids graduate from college with debt that they might never be able to pay off? This is an earth-shattering situation. We never think it will happen to us. While you are employed, you should still prepare for your next job or career. When you go to school–a wonderful, blessed opportunity–you better think about what you will do after graduation to earn a living or how you are going to pivot from where you are today.

I met a 55-year-old cook in a pizza parlor who had been a struggling piano player doing gigs in Nashville. Now, after many years, a friend who is a state trooper told him that there is a shortage of correction officers: good pay, training, benefits, a pension, and flexible hours. It sounds perfect because he can also still make pizzas part-time.

There is a need for more prison guards, because there are more prisons and more people going to jail. Currently, the United States is the world's leader in incarceration with 2.2 million people currently in the nation's prisons and jails, a 500% increase over the last 40 years. Changes in sentencing law and policy, not changes in crime rates, explain most of this increase. Another trend.

It's a proven fact that the more education you have, the more money you will earn over your lifetime. Yet plenty of college-educated employees often don't pay attention to the trends that will affect them. You should be aware if you are in a shrinking field, and if your skills are transferable to a growing field, consider switching.

I published books. I moved into magazines. I published

print, then CD-ROM arrived: I moved into CD-ROM and then left print entirely. Next I moved into the internet, when it appeared. Then software. Each time I had to learn new skills. But I was not alone. Millions of people learned much more than I will ever know about coding and digital applications (apps) and technology marketing, etc. Follow the trends.

If you are going to be entrepreneurial, you have to pay attention to what people are willing to pay for. Almost 20 years ago, I heard a heartening story about a 65-year-old man with no education who sold his business in 1998 for $66 million.

He was a big, burly guy who started in the Bronx hanging onto the back of a garbage truck. When it stopped, he had the brawn to pick up the full cans and heave them into the truck. His boss did the driving. One day he decided that he was smarter than his boss, so he borrowed a few dollars from his grandma, and ended up with his own truck and next his own customers. The success was only temporary.

A Mafia don named Albert Anastasia (who ran Murder, Inc.!) took his truck and said, "You can't be here. This is MY territory. LEAVE! But here's some money, so you can take your family and start over somewhere else." (That was very nice of Albert!)

The garbage collector moved to Hartford, CT and became the King of Trash there!

I was always inspired by this story. And I never forgot it. There must have been a lot of hard work to build up a company worth that much. It takes managing employees, payroll, satisfying government regulations, fighting off competitors, taking bank loans to buy trucks. On and on. But it's clearly possible.

Can you imagine anything in your town or neighborhood that people are going to always need that doesn't take large amounts of capital to get started? You will only find it if you look. Or bump into it by accident and recognize it. Learning about trends that are affecting you and others will give you a huge edge up in deciding if your job or business idea is in a growing field.

Just don't think that the expansion will continue forever.

CHAPTER TWELVE
PERKS OF TRAUMA

Trauma always causes change. That is the silver lining to a big blow of an event, assuming you aren't totally beaten down by the event, and you are one of those who can make lemonade out of lemons. You can learn and benefit from these terrible and painful experiences.

If it isn't a true life crisis, and just a little bump in the road, you may still have a different view after the fact. So what kind of major upsets am I talking about? A list like this one from Healthline[19] is easy to compile and can be greatly expanded:

Death of Family Member, Friend, Teacher, or Pet	Natural Disaster, Such as a Flood, Tornado, or Fire	Witnessing a Death or Another Traumatic Event
Divorce	Terrorism	Rape
Physical Pain or Injury	Moving to a New Location	Domestic Abuse
Illness	Parental Abandonment	Prison Stay
War		Loss of Job
		Bankruptcy

There is another list of stress-related events that can be linked to illness and weighted by severity according to the Holmes and Rahe Scale.

Some of these in order of most stressful are: (see next page).

You probably noticed that some of these can be positive events, like marriage and pregnancy, assuming it's not a shotgun wedding and the pregnancy is with someone you love. It is also worth noting how relatively low on both lists are the money and job related changes, like firing, financial loss and bankruptcy.

LIFE EVENT	LIFE CHANGE UNITS
Death of a spouse	100
Divorce	73
Marital separation	65
Imprisonment	63
Death of a close family member	63
Personal injury or illness	53
Marriage	50
Dismissal from work	47
Marital reconciliation	45
Retirement	45
Change in health of family member	44
Pregnancy	40
Sexual difficulties	39
Gain a new family member	39
Business readjustment	39
Change in financial state	38
Death of a close friend	37
Change to different line of work	36
Change in frequency of arguments	35
Major mortgage	32
Foreclosure of mortgage or loan	30

When you look over these two lists, it's no wonder people are so confronted much of the time. It is no wonder when they are ill or anxious, rattled and fearful. It might seem like almost everyone is affected by the life events listed here, and there are many more items that could be included. Just google "trauma" and "stress" to see what I mean.

Maybe you also better understand now why people drink or are angry, hostile, argumentative, depressed, moping, lack enthusiasm, etc. Life is suffering (the Buddhists say), and "Life is difficult" are the opening words of M. Scott Peck's bestselling book, *The Road Less Traveled*.

I also heard growing up that "adversity is what makes 'real' people and builds character." To that I felt forced to add: If you were lucky enough to survive it. At my 20th high school reunion, when classmates were around 38, I could see a number who had been beaten up badly by life. Some looked destroyed. I was told that many who didn't show were in even worse shape. Those were in the group that had met adversity that crushed them. They had not been hardened positively, like the sword in the hottest flame.

They had melted.

On the other hand, those who survive the fires and poundings of life are more confident, though warier. They know where to be cautious, how to avoid some traps, are not as smug as when they lacked experience. They are also more knowledgeable about how to avoid pitfalls, and find the easier paths. Lessons were learned. They had survived for the moment.

One of my high school classmates told me at our 55th reunion that he "never thought that he'd be dealing with divorce at this point in his life." In my case, it was the same year that my 44-year-old daughter had divorced.

It never ends. We all have some of these traumas, crises and stresses. If you haven't had any yet, you are unbelievably fortunate, lucky, one in a million. However, I promise you, they will come. Hopefully, you are somewhat prepared emotionally, but also much better prepared financially. You might have some savings. Or already started acquiring new skills. Have you reduced or eliminated debt?

When I first visited Japan on the way to my 13-month army tour in Korea, I hired a student guide in Tokyo who wanted some money and practice in English. When we sat on the bus he gripped the floor-to-ceiling pole so hard, and braced both feet toward the front so firmly, I asked him about it. I never forgot his answer, "In case the bus crashes, I want to be ready." I asked if he had been in a crash before, and he hadn't, he was just preparing for it, just in case.

There must be millions of people who live their lives braced for the tragedies they are sure will come. It must make them tense, fearful and lessen their joy of living. I knew a grown man who went hiking and fell off the mountain to his death; another photographer friend died taking pictures of a glacier in Alaska. It is smart to be aware. Shit happens.

In fact, my real message in this chapter is that it is going to happen to you. More than once. Your life will bump into one of those items listed earlier. It will be a bitch. You may be maimed, you may cry, feel sorry for yourself, ask God "Why me?" But I guarantee you, some of those bad days are ahead. I hope sincerely that you never experience the horrible misfortunes. Yet it's certainly possible.

What I want to emphasize is that these catastrophes and hurdles have some unexpected benefits. Silver linings. Maybe gold or platinum. Because after the shock and sadness and setbacks and loss and forced adjustments and regrets and self-pity (even if it is justified), you are forever different.

If, and this is a big if, you are not destroyed or crushed by these normal, almost every day, life events, you are no longer the person you used to be with the attitudes and anxieties you used to have. You might be more apprehensive and live braced for the next crisis. However, if you have suffered the death of a spouse or someone close to you, how can you possibly become upset the next time you receive a traffic ticket or are served steak a bit too rare.

This is the benefit that I see in living...and surviving stronger from crisis. It seems so easy to me to rationalize now that the little stuff is meaningless, next to the big stuff you experienced.

When I married the second time, two women I dated earlier were dead, as was my wife's first husband. Both of us had survived these losses, sadder but wiser. The little things just couldn't affect us the same way they might have years earlier, before our loved ones had passed. Sharing these values about 'what really matters' has made our marriage bonds better. We do not freak out, when there is a small problem that costs a few dollars, someone says something disparaging or insulting. We might not ignore it. We might respond to it, but often our response is calm and controlled.

I am not a Buddha, guru or religious leader. I do not have most of the answers, but I do see that encounters and hurdles that bother others are often easy for me to sidestep emotionally. Sometimes I feel obliged to 'fight' back. I know I can do it from a place of justice or right/wrong, and often with a laugh to defuse or ridicule the offender.

Don't misunderstand my point, if I lost all my money and was forced to downsize, beg, live on charity, I'd be miserable. But I don't live each day as if I am entitled to the standard of living I now enjoy, and that it will continue forever. I'd like that, of course, but 'life' happens. I play tennis gleefully each week, knowing that one turn or misstep, and my tennis-playing days could be ended.

I enjoy my health and pay attention to diet and exercise, because I know that it could be over in a minute. I was in a three-car accident on the way home. One car on the highway at rush hour crashed into the car behind me, and that car collided into my rear end. The first car was totaled. Luckily none of the three little girls, or anyone else in all our cars, was hurt. I have also been in two other accidents in which my cars were totaled.

When life is so fragile, so fleeting, how can you not know

and recall these realities and do everything in your power to adjust your attitude about living? I know it's easy to say and hard to change. Rational thinking has little to do with the emotional reactions of that lizard brain still buried deep within each of our heads.

A few traumas or crises will give you the opportunity to modify your outlook. Unfortunately, you will have these catastrophes. Fortunately, after some time and healing and acceptance of what you went through, there are perks also buried deep in these bad moments. You may have to dig and search to locate them and integrate them into your way of being. They are like precious jewels that need to be uncovered. You have to recognize their potential. You may have to shine them up with mental effort. You may have to cut some facets away, or learn how to chip them to make them brilliant.

It's all there waiting for you. No charge. Yours for the taking. Easier said than done, but do-able. Maybe you can do it. Why not? Others have. If they can, maybe you can. That is what inspirational stories are all about: to show you the way, to give you hope and methods of following those before you and walking similar paths.

By the time I was 40, I had had three major setbacks that upset me. I wasn't clinically depressed, not even nearly, but I was in a bad place. Time passed, I survived each blow. Maybe the first time was contracting hepatitis in Korea, coming home on a stretcher and spending weeks in hospitals and recuperating at home. The second time a dozen years later was my separation and eventual divorce. The third time was after losing all my money and then being fired. But I survived. Somehow, I was not destroyed by these disasters. In fact, reading a book about divorce that a new friend gave me helped me feel that I was no longer all alone. I was part of a new group of millions of divorced men. I had a new community of brothers I could talk to and share with, and I have been helping newly divorced guys I meet for decades since then.

The fourth time I had a catastrophe, I remembered that I'd felt okay months after the first three traumas. I had confidence that "this too will pass." I will again survive this latest crisis, and I did, in less time than the earlier agonies. I had been changed by the fire. Tempered with a better outlook. I knew I would be okay.

I once read that we live in psychological bubbles that make it easier for us to deal with daily life. When we have trauma or extreme stress, these 'bubbles' burst open, and we can see the whole world anew. We are open to change, we have lots of coincidences, good things also happen. For 50-years I thought I'd read that in a book by Alvin Toffler called *Future Shock*, but when I finally relocated that book from my storage, I couldn't find the references. Nevertheless, the concept makes sense to me.

In a related view, a psychologist I met once who applied for my part-time, advertising space sales opening, told me it helps to recognize that people have so much to deal with that they can't take in too much new information.

Buying ad space for potential advertisers is "another stimulus," she informed me, and that is often too difficult to handle. Sounds like those bubbles I just mentioned, doesn't it? Salespeople must keep on calling prospects until they find some who are open to change, and then maybe one or two will be just ripe for a deal.

However most of us are in our protective cocoons, struggling to fend off the overwhelmingness of our normal lives. When harsh circumstances crack open those barriers, we are forced to deal with the stresses we have. Then we are forever changed and have the opportunity to live our lives differently.

William Blake wrote poems about how experience teaches us. Yet the lessons cost us our innocence. It is a price worth paying in some cases. Hopefully, you can exploit your trials and hurdles, and find the kernels of light in your darkness.

It may take a brush or a shovel to unearth the choice bits of your trauma. Dig away. Remove that dirt and move on to a better life. It's all possible, and you have the power to create the will to do it. Are you ready to begin? Why not start immediately? Small steps. One by one.

You can do it. I am sure of it. Many others have done it before you. It takes effort. Everyone has a past that makes it harder than one might think. Especially you. Nevertheless, I am totally optimistic, because you have read this far. You have the want and will to consider change. Keep reading, and I will suggest some techniques that simplify the whole process.

CHAPTER THIRTEEN

START-UPS

There is a fabulous way to make spectacular returns solely by investing your money: start-ups. You are taking extraordinary risk, of course. That's part of the bargain: big risk, big potential reward. Small safe risk leads to minimal reward. In this game, you must have the temperament to be willing to fail, to lose everything, to not take it personally and to not be miserable that you are a screw up for making a mistake.

Starting up your own business is not what I am referring to here. I mean investing in someone else's idea and backing an individual who may be a stranger, and doing it early on. If you put in some of the very first money or as part of the earliest round of funds from family and friends, that's called angel investing. It is light years before venture capitalists (VCs) would ever consider putting in their millions and reputations.

Sometimes there is only an idea in a conversation or on an envelope, no PowerPoint slide show or 30-50-page executive summary and business plan. It's a real crap shoot, and the majority of these start-ups will fail or produce no returns for investors. When I started my publishing business in 1977, I read that 90% of new companies are defunct after three years.

These days I can only find stats that say 50% of new businesses will fail after five years, so the odds have improved. That is good news. Even today the estimates are that eventually 80% of all new businesses will fail.

One possible explanation for this difference may be how a new business is defined. I think the current facts are based on incorporated start-ups and those with more than just one employee. Regardless, you can see how difficult it is to succeed in creating a successful venture. Plus, when you are merely the investor, you aren't doing the day-to-day work that would give you more control. So you have to make a huge judgment about the likelihood of success by the people you are backing.

I read that only 2-6% of start-ups in general ever seek venture capital investment, and that only 0.2-2% receive it. One Silicon Valley VC believes a much larger portion, maybe a majority, of young tech companies come looking for VC money, and 2-5% of those are lucky enough to be funded that way. Another told me that his firm funds just one out of every 500 pitches they hear! That's the 0.2%. These are very small numbers. Although the results of VC firms aren't widely publicized, there are some general ranges you can glean. Overall 80-90% do not return a profit. Even after all the high-priced due diligence and experienced analysis and review of hundreds of possibilities. I heard that six out of 10 lose all the money. Three out of 10 make no money, but return the original investment and one makes a ton of money. The ratio is 6-3-1.

A second source claimed the ratio is closer to 4-4-2, and two very successful VC managers who specializes only in high tech start-ups told me directly that their firm's ratio is 5-4-1 in one case and 3-3-3 in the other.

I am alerting you right from the start that the odds are against your making money with this approach. These are the small businesses that make up the bulk of growth in the economy. They are the success stories that are publicized and whose founders are praised and admired.

The possibilities are real.

Nevertheless, I have concluded that maybe one in 1000 or, at best, one in 200 of the earliest-stage, angel investment technology start-ups that eventually receive VC funding will ever make a big profit. Reaching profitably has to be that difficult or harder for the non-technology businesses. Remember, over 94% of general start-ups never want or receive VC funding. They are financed by rich individuals, family funds and other businesses that believe in them.

It's all very speculative at those earliest stages. You are betting on a situation long before there is a business or any revenues. No staff, no office. You are simply backing a long-shot dark horse in a race against the proven winners who are already on the track. Sometimes you are looking for an idea that is so new that the field is just opening, with few or no competitors. This is why I like high tech businesses that will totally transform an industry or start a new one. It is called Disruptive Technology.

The term angel investing has gained in popularity in recent years and is often used interchangeably with the term start-up investing. There are even mutual funds you can invest in now that will only place your money in several early-stage start-ups. These are usually companies without revenues, but with a staff, an office and a product that is partially developed. Maybe these young firms have already spent their initial angel funding and are back for more. This is way past the angel stage in my view, but that's a minor distinction. The possible returns suggested in these later rounds might be four to seven times what you risk over a three to five-year period.

What these funds and the VC companies have in common is that the start-ups looking for money know about them and come in droves to make presentations that will persuade the funds and VCs to invest. The companies with the money appear to have time pressure to invest their money and are also hoping that if they invest in enough new businesses that one or three of them will be giant successes.

I am less impressed with this model and the relatively small reward. I know that four to seven times returns aren't so small, compared to two to 10% a year in bonds or stocks. Even so, I like the very earliest stage opportunities, true angels, where you can receive 25 or 100 times returns. But these successes are incredibly rare. No matter, I have taken these risks and find them the most exciting, creative and satisfying. I love offering advice and support to the founders one or more times a week in the beginning, less often as the business grows, and staff and outside professionals are located and affordable.

I should also admit that only one of my angel investments has been a success to date. Five failed completely: all that money is gone. However, 10 others, a mix of angels and early-stage, are still alive, and some are looking extremely promising, though most are not yet profitable, even after five to ten years. You better be patient, not need the money, and be willing to lose it all.

You also might want to read stories by investors with more successful histories. Although my wife and I hit one ultra-grand slammer with Take Two, I hope our limited record convinces you that little guys like us, and maybe you, can still make a go of it. We are still a small-potatoes, mom and pop operation. Not everyone finds a Google, Facebook or PayPal.

I can't emphasize enough that the most important determinant of whether the start-up will become a profitable business is the founder. You are betting on this visionary who has a dream that he or she wants to implement with your money. You must size up this individual just as carefully as the idea and its market. Great idea, great opportunity and poor manager or non-leader, and you are doomed to fail and will lose your investment.

I have watched one friend expend two years of time and money attempting to create a business that would be run by an associate he knew was immoral. My friend lost everything. I have seen good managers fail with concepts that appeared worthless to me. One often encounters the scientist or geek with a fabulous idea or invention, but no business experience. Or another founder, formerly a top executive in a large corporation, lacks familiarity with a start-up, where there is limited staff or money to carry out the most menial tasks that were handled by lower-level employees at her previous company.

Start noticing traits of people who succeed in running a small company. How well you can size up the person you give your funds to will make almost all the difference at the end. It will determine whether your return is zero or a number followed by many zeroes.

Don't be swayed by friendship or family connections. Those relationships might introduce you to the opportunity, but should have no bearing on your ultimate decision, unless the person you are backing already has a proven, successful track record. I read recently that angel investors put money into 10% of the deals they look at, but venture capital firms only invest in 0.2-2% of their applicants. Be cautious with your money. Don't let friendship and family persuade you to risk your hard-earned, saved-with-difficulty dollars.

My past results have convinced people to invest in some of my later deals. Similarly, I have invested in projects brought to me by others who have generated good returns earlier. After three or four projects, I recognized that I had morphed into an "angel investor," and I met others with funds and similar, high-risk temperaments.

I will never say, "If I could do it, you can do it." This game is very speculative, you are not in control, you can lose everything. However, I will do my best to expose you to how the game is played, so that you can better understand if it is an arena you'd like to explore.

Let me tell you about three of my start-up investments, so you can understand my role and how these investments happen. They sometimes involve flukes, accidents, intuition and luck. Nothing you can count on, but approaches you should look out for and seize instantly when you bump into them. I have the impression that stories like mine are not uncommon, even when you learn how random and haphazard some aspects of them are.

When I was publishing my annual picture books, I went to the first five TED conferences to learn about some of the latest technological developments. They were amazing five-day gatherings attended by geniuses and visionaries: speakers like Bill Gates, Steve Jobs, the president of Adobe, the man who invented hyperlink, the scientist behind the first computer recognition voice software. I was one of the first 3000 people in the world to experience virtual reality, we heard about the first GPS system for cars. Astonishing. There was a 4 3/4-inch, silver disc called a CD-ROM that we heard about and that I thought was perfect for my business: it could store all the photos I was printing on paper that comprised a book weighing 3-5 pounds.

I made one somehow, but there was a major problem: there weren't many CD-ROM drives in existence yet, under one million in the entire United States.

At the same time, people wanted to buy my company, so I was meeting with suitors set up by an investment banking firm, Veronis Suhler, that specialized in media firms. It had sold TV Guide for $2 billion, which was a lot in those days. At a meeting, I had with an older, top exec from ABC Publishing, I told him about my idea for making CD-ROMs. When the session was over, Don the banker who had arranged the meeting, critiqued my performance: "Didn't you see the buyer's eyes roll, when you mentioned that CD, whatever you called it. Don't ever mention that Buck Rogers stuff again. He thought you were a bit looney."

I never received an offer I couldn't resist, that buyer eventually went out of business, and six months after that ABC meeting, in 1993, Don called me to say he had a 21-year-old kid in his office who was looking for a partner to invest in CD-ROMs. He thought of me right away, and I practically said, "Yes!" over the phone.

It was intuitive, felt so right, so natural and easy. It didn't bother me to learn later that the kid's father made tens of millions a year, according to his son, but didn't believe in the new business idea and wouldn't be the first to invest; nor that the father had spent time in prison after being charged with tax problems. This should have been more than enough to keep me away, according to my lawyer.

My wife and I went in with our eyes wide open, and before long, I think I heard that 29 of the 50 CD-ROMs Apple was distributing were from the company that Ryan and I had created. It was amazing, and they were mostly about exotic travel overseas. I was merely a small-time publisher who had bought some tickets to a handful of TED conferences, and here I was in the business of helping make nationally distributed CD-ROMs. Ryan was running our company day-to-day, while I still managed my publishing company and gave him frequent business advice based on my 15 years of entrepreneurship.

Then two unrelated events came together magically, unpredictably, and unimaginably. However, this is one of the common unexpected directions I believe most businesses and much of life takes. If you stay in the game long enough, things will happen that you could never anticipate. You have a new opportunity, sometimes after a debilitating setback or disappointment. You must be flexible and adapt to the changed or questionable circumstances.

The first event was Ryan coming to my house with his girlfriend, showing my wife and me what Mario Brothers games were all about and declaring that he wanted to pivot (today's word, not back then), or shift into gaming. He believed it had wider appeal and would grow much more substantially. No argument. We all agreed and launched into this new direction.

The second fluke was that I had invested in another start-up called PT Mouse that some affluent friends had raved about (all our money was lost when the company went bust) that was creating a computer mouse that could operate in the air, no desk or firm surface needed, perfect for an airplane mechanic under a wing outdoors. I gave the founder one of my CD-ROMs, which were quite novel back then.

Weeks later, I received a call from the founder's friend who was visiting from London. He had seen my CD-ROM and was wondering how to make his own CD, because he was in a rock band and wanted to make a demo. As we talked, I learned that his full-time job was working as a global headhunter for high-tech companies.

Meanwhile, Ryan had been complaining that he couldn't find any people with gaming experience to help us move into that field. So I asked this new acquaintance in London if he knew anyone who had made computer games before. To my amazement he said, "As a matter of fact, a company in Pennsylvania was just sold that had a gaming division of 11 people that the buyer did not acquire. These people are now looking for jobs."

I told this news to Ryan, he had our company buy the whole division for almost nothing, and our reoriented business was off and running. Today that company we started is one the most well-known game companies in the world, is publicly traded and in 2018 was valued at around $15 billion.

You can see the succession of events that led to this result. If you read it in a novel, you would say that it couldn't possibly be believable—too far-fetched and unlikely. The drama of how Ryan and other execs backdated options and were punished and fined by the SEC would also be too improbable, as well as how they distorted some accounting rules to make the company's operating results appear better than they were.

Nevertheless, it was a very successful investment that none of my friends took a chance on. In fact, they and my professional advisors thought I was crazy to risk funds in the field and with the venture's partners. In the end my overall joint investment with my wife returned about 14 times what we risked, and some of the earlier monies generated much higher returns. Despite the PT Mouse loss, the game company win inspired me to try other start-ups that might work out well, and you can see that the Mouse failure was instrumental in the success of the game company, which is called Take Two Interactive Software. This company owns all rights to the Grand Theft Auto franchise, which has sold about 325 million copies, and owns at least nine other titles that sell more than five million copies with each new sequel.

The video game industry is now approaching $135 billion annually, much more than the Hollywood movie industry. It is our dominant cultural medium and the fastest-growing entertainment segment. This was not the least bit obvious 20 years ago. Critics thought it was a limited distraction for teenage boys and geeks. Today the average gamer is 37, and 42% of gamers are female. People completely missed this revolution. I have no idea why the field looked so promising to me. I never play video games, never did beyond a couple of the simplest ones with my kids.

But I did have the intuition to make CD-ROMs, and I trusted

that feeling, as well as the shift into gaming urged by my 21-year-old partner. These hunches were completely inexplicable and irrational. However, my wife and I had them and were willing to risk big on them.

In 2005, I again had a certain intuition, triggered by a local weekly paper news story about a design studio 45 minutes away that worked with computers and had young innovative staffers. I called there to see if my computer-enthusiast son, Gavin, 15, could come by once a week after school and learn how computers were used in the business world to make designs, images and animations. They agreed to let him come in.

During the next year, Gavin sat at someone's desk a couple of hours a week watching the creative process in action and invented a simple video game that he loaded on the net. The game generated publicity and comments from many countries around the world. "It should be on a smartphone," we heard frequently, so I signed on as my son's agent and made inquiries without success for five months.

One day, I thought to ask the head of the design studio, where Gavin was now "interning," one afternoon a week, and he passed me on to a client who knew someone who bought games for cell phones. I called Ben Davis cold, made my pitch, and asked to learn more about his company. He sent me a printed prospectus prepared to raise money that had info about Ben, his co-founder and their firm's long-range plans. As soon as we next spoke, I said I might be interested in investing.

Ben informed me that they'd already received an offer to buy the company, but he had another proposal for me that

Ben Davis. CEO of Phizzle.

was even better. He was right. He came out from San Francisco to see me in New York. He gave me his presentation at the 7 Stars Restaurant. After coming to terms, I wired $12,500 to him and also to his tech partner, Max Woon.

Max had already designed one of the most popular websites in the world at that time, which was very persuasive in convincing me to take the risk. Years later I learned that Max used some of my wife's and my funds to move off his friend's couch, rent his own apartment, and buy a new computer. Within two years, Viacom bought Max's popular X-fire site for $104 million, and Max's share made him a multi-millionaire. He then became less interested in the business I had invested in.

What was the idea? A version of Twitter, before there was Twitter, with one enormous difference: it would be voice messaging to cell phones, rather than text. But that proved to be a deadly distinction. Back then, the idea of making one call to reach tens of thousands of traveling cell phones was a complicated and breakthrough technological achievement. Max could do it, and we all also saw that cell phones might become portable computers. Remember, this was before laptops and tablets. Nevertheless, voice protocol had too many limitations, and Ben couldn't make the business model successful.

We switched to text after about two years, by which time we were one of many firms in the field. We had lost our early-entry advantage in the market. But Ben, age 35 when we met, had other ideas that grew out of his younger days as a semi-pro basketball player in London. What if we focused on the sports market and offered our software tailored specifically to sports teams and arenas that want to offer their fans and audiences a more interactive experience?

Well it was a brilliant insight, and before long we were hired by the Cleveland Cavaliers, beat out 17 competitors to be chosen by Madison Square Garden, were written up in 2010 by *The New York Times*. After that we were included in a *Forbes Magazine* list of America's hot upcoming companies and became established as a major fan engagement provider in the sports industry. Over the next few years, we raised $15 million in VC money and then pivoted into a big data company that analyzed the demographics of sports team fans better than anyone.

We have partnered with Twitter (covered the World Cup 2014), Fox Sports, the software giant SAP, Cisco and many others. Our company, called Phizzle, looks like it is going to be a success. It has software it has created that no one else in the world can offer. I still can't grasp how our little start-up arrived at this point. Ben deserves most of the credit of course. He stuck it out, he adapted, he built the team and found the technical geniuses to bring us to this level.

As you have surely recognized by now, investing in a

start-up run by someone else demands your total faith that this stranger: is committed, is smart enough to shift in a changing market, can overcome all the obstacles and setbacks and disappointments that will definitely burden him or her, can manage limited funds, can raise new funds, can communicate clearly with other potential investors, inspire staff, relate to technical types or industrial designers, be a Renaissance man or woman in countless other ways, etc. Ben is such a person, so here we are at last. Looking good, great, unbelievable.

It's only been 15 years, so far. Not exactly an overnight success, and there has been lots of grief, hurdles and low cash flow. It's nothing like the movies or the stories of Facebook's almost instant success and the rapid victories of other famous firms now worth billions. Forget about that fantasy. Phizzle's survival to this point has often been an agony and a constant worry. But that is how it happens sometimes. Probably most times. Hopefully there will be an exit within the next few years, and the payoff will be the 50-plus multiple that we initial investors pray for. Once again, I helped nurture and find money for this start-up, while providing guidance and suggestions in the early days of the company's existence. It's one of the most exciting, creative and satisfying experiences I have enjoyed.

It all started with my teenage son inventing a simple video game that might play on a cell phone plus a connection from a design studio I read about in a weekly, small-town newspaper. Could it be any more random? Just trust your intuition and have dollars saved that you can risk. I know some people think it takes courage and a willingness to take on more uncertainty in a world already too complicated and broadcasting fear and danger abounding every second. You can't do this stuff if the additional stress is too upsetting. I have friends with millions of dollars who would never miss $50-100,000. However, they are terrified of making a humiliating mistake or of adding anxiety to their already fluttering stomachs.

I wanted to share a little of the process, even if it is too confronting for you. Perhaps, you will be able to adapt these anecdotes into your investment strategies. The most important thing to take away is to recognize the intuitive feelings in your brain, your heart or your gut that should be listened to.

A third example was right in line with this philosophy. In this case, I want to describe a much more common way to invest in start-ups—through angel groups. There are hundreds of investor groups that specialize in various aspects of the start-up field. Golden Seeds focuses on new companies founded or run by women. Tech Coast Angels in LA focuses on tech and science companies in southern California. You can join one of these groups, be introduced to the start-ups seeking funds from them and talk over the potential of each pitch with fellow investors. So figure out what areas or industries appeal to you and join an angel group that meshes with your interests.

One of our journeys started with my wife's long-term love of science and outer space. Jacqueline says that as a child she even dreamt of becoming an astronaut. So it's no surprise that decades later, when she was doing her research of start-ups to invest in, she explored the new space—or private spaceflight—industry and quickly learned about a young organization called Space Angels.

We both joined, acquired access to the deal flow screened

out by the Space Angels administrators and made a few investments in companies we both liked. In some cases we have visited the headquarters of these firms and established ongoing relationships with the founders. You might not realize how much activity is taking place here, but $23.6 billion of private money has poured into this field since 2009, and $5.3 billion in 2019 alone. Originally government multi-billions were needed to launch huge rockets carrying humans. Then billionaires using their private fortunes built SpaceX (Elon Musk) and Blue Origin (Jeff Bezos), broke into this government market, created competition, and that led to lower costs and greater innovation.

However analog satellites that used to be the size of a bus can now be digital satellites as small as a loaf of bread. You don't need to wait three years to hitch your satellite a ride on a 230-foot, $90 million rocket from SpaceX. Instead you can use a 56-foot, $5.7 million rocket from Rocket Lab devoted to your microsatellite in just a few months. It's a new entrepreneurial space age and highly innovative.

So Iceye invented a small satellite that uses radar not an optical camera and can function at night and through clouds. Atlas Space is building ground stations that can retrieve and analyze the digital data being collected. World View builds stratospheric balloons that can hover over a specific area of the Earth for weeks delivering imagery for a fraction of a satellite's cost. And the values of some of these companies have increased over 10 times in three years.

Money aside, one of the greatest thrills in business is watching or being part of the creative process. Seeing the pictures of the products being built and savoring the videos of test flights is breathtaking. Especially knowing that you as an investor helped make it all possible.

We have all heard stories about entrepreneurs like Elon Musk who risk all they own and more to make their businesses succeed. Sometimes they go into debt, suffer broken marriages, endure terrible anxiety and sickness.

I have not taken those chances in this case, and neither should you, when you are investing in others. But big rewards demand huge risks. I encourage you to take them, when you have that feeling of rightness, and you have some extra money you can afford to lose.

One final point: success in this arena usually takes a long time. You should accept that it is rarely achieved instantly, right away, within the first couple of years. You read and hear about those fortunate few. You learn about lottery winners too. But your odds are infinitesimal. Starting a business takes a lot of work. Owners need to refine the concept, develop the product or service, win over customers, wait for the word about the business to spread, adapt to changing conditions and demands in the market. If you accept this view, you are less likely to become discouraged as time marches on, and the results you hoped for, believed in, remain elusive.

Having patience and realistic expectations will help you through your investment's tough times. You can also be a welcome support, advisor and cheerleader to the executives you bet on. I am always amazed as I talk to the founders or top managers of companies I invest in to learn how few of the other investors call the CEO or comment in writing on the latest business update. My calls always seem to be appreciated, and I always learn more than was sent out in the mass mailing. It renews my optimism and gives me more faith in our chances of success. Stay involved, and the rewards will be greater than monetary.

CHAPTER FOURTEEN

COINCIDENCE

I want to talk now about subjects that are much more controversial, disputable, and unscientific. However, I know from my personal experience that there is something going on here. It is very true and powerful and has changed my life in numerous ways, brought me happiness and money and career success, a wonderful marriage and a better (though questionable) understanding of how the world works.

I expect you to be skeptical. I know that many people will be dismissive and will even think me a nutcase. But if you have read this far, try to have an open mind and at least scan this chapter. What do you have to lose, besides a few minutes of reading?

After I separated from my first wife, I started noticing a lot more coincidences in my daily life. It was weird and inexplicable. We all have them, you can read about others' stories online and in books. But what causes them, and what are they good for?

The explanations are somewhat fanciful, but not very explanatory. Often, they are descriptive and anecdotal. But no scientific evidence to support a theory. Nevertheless, they clearly happen.

Intuitions and hunches are also mysterious 'inclinations' to do something or take a path. In addition, there is an area of psychology called "psi" phenomena that encompasses four different kinds of events:

Precognition—foretelling the future.

Remote sensing/viewing—your mind travels to some other physical location and can report what it 'sees.'

Telepathy/clairvoyance—you can communicate with another

human (maybe even an animal) who is too far away to hear or see you.

Psychokinesis—making an object move without touching it.

I or others I know and trust completely have had some of these experiences. They have been very beneficial. So listen a bit and see what you think. I may be unusually sensitive, and you are not. I am certainly not a psychic who can predict the future at will, tell you your future, find missing persons and help detectives solve murders. But some of this stuff has happened to me, people I know, or was caused by me. I heard three stories in my family that were pretty powerful:

1. My mother woke up during the Second World War and said, "Arthur (her husband, my father) has been hit." Six weeks later, she received a letter explaining that on the precise day she had that startle, my father was dropping depth charges on a submarine, and one of them exploded prematurely. He took some shrapnel in his leg.

2. After growing up some of his younger years near Los Angeles, my father moved to Florida and returned to California just once after maybe 60 years. He drives up the coast through Big Sur and eats at the outdoor community tables at Nepenthe Restaurant overlooking the Pacific. An old guy he talks to was the cinematographer of the movie Cimarron (1931). My father says that as a 21-year-old, he was an extra in that movie driving a wagon pulled by horses during the land rush scene.

3. My father made his only trip to a kibbutz in Israel, woke up before breakfast and went to the mess hall, where one woman was preparing food. They talked, he said where he was from and where Anna, his mother, grew up: Ukraine.

"Where in Ukraine?" "Near Kiev," he answered. "Where near Kiev?" "Near Zhytomyr." "Where exactly?" "In a very little town near Zhytomyr called Novohrad-Volynskyi, which used to be called Zvhil." "Anna with the red hair?" In 2013, this town had a population of 56,000. Yet my father woke up to meet a woman in Israel who played with Anna as a small girl.

I live today in a town of just 1400 people, so what are the odds that a man with my identical first and last name would move here? But he did, he is the architect, and I am the publisher Ira.

As a kid and pre-marriage-separated adult, I didn't pay much attention to how coincidences occur. I did what all of us usually do to explain these "flukes": merely say "it was just a coincidence." This explains absolutely nothing.

Two moths that want to mate are miles apart yet they come together and reproduce. How is that possible? Is this a coincidence? No. Scientists have conducted experiments and proven that the female emits a chemical, a pheromone, that the unbelievably, super sensitive smelling male can detect even seven miles away. We have a logical, scientifically demonstrated explanation to something about moths mating, but still no insights regarding human coincidences.

We don't give conclusions like these about moths a second thought. Other than being astonished and impressed that the moths can do it. But if we didn't know about the pheromone, we would be mystified.

Suppose coincidences, intuition and psi events are analogous: there is a clear way for these human occurrences and accidents to be explained, it's just that scientists haven't yet figured them out. However, these inexplicable phenomena happen, and whether we understand the *How* of the experience, we might be able to benefit from—and even exploit—the existence of these common events in our personal lives.

Some writers say that coincidences are simply random accidents that we give some meaning to by attaching a special confluence of personal connections. This is totally arbitrary.

For example, I was reading a *Time Magazine* in the dentist's office and an article mentioned Larry Tisch, who owned hotels and CBS at the time. I looked at the photo of him in the magazine and then realized that the only other person right opposite me in the waiting room was Larry Tisch. Twenty years later, I am complaining to my friend Joe while eating dinner at Lindy's restaurant before seeing a show on Broadway: the food is poor quality, and only tourists come. We should choose another place next time. Half an hour later I look at the table across from me—it is a big restaurant, and I am against the wall at a two-person table—and there is Larry Tisch with his family. I go over and tell them how they proved me wrong about only tourists eating there, then I tell them the *Time Magazine* story, and they laugh for a second time.

I put photos of my family cutting a Christmas tree in Connecticut on my high school website, and Bryna Williams writes how great we look, and that she wishes she was still living in Litchfield, CT, where she rented a house for 12 months in the 70s. "Which house?" I write back, because the town only has 8000 people in it. She describes it by name, an historic colonial built in 1786. Two days later, I visit my close friends at the time for dinner and discover that their house is the one Bryna lived in. I write back to her from the house using my friend's computer.

In 1958, I was a freshman in college, a chemistry major. I was dating Jeannie Peters, a drama major. We broke up a year after we started dating. Shortly, after our break-up she started dating another drama student, Jamie Cromwell, who "understands her better." We lose touch after graduation. Twenty years later, my girlfriend Marilyn and I visit her pregnant friend Ginger in Oregon. Nothing imminent, so we drive down to Los Angeles and share the cost of a room at her upscale hotel choice, the Chateau Marmont. After a couple of days, Ginger goes into labor, Marilyn flies right up to Oregon, I can't afford to pay for the room myself and am sitting in it alone on a Friday afternoon wondering where I am going to spend the night.

The phone rings: it's Marilyn's LA friend from Yale drama returning her call. I ask him to recommend a hotel. He says he is out of town, and I can stay at his place on one of the Canyon roads. Next morning I look through his books. He is a director or producer and has won an Academy Award for a documentary about the hip, roller skating scene at Venice, CA. One of his books has the names and pictures of actors and their agents. My college girlfriend Jeannie is included. I decide to call the listed number, which is for her agent...who picks up and says how lucky I am that he unexpectedly had to go to his office on a Saturday.

I tell him my story, he agrees to call Jeannie, and she calls me within 10 minutes. We talk for over an hour, I ask her if we can have a drink or dinner, she says not until Sunday night. I ask her where she lives, so I can pick her up...and she is four houses away from me right on the road I am staying on.

We meet the next night, eat sushi, catch up, enjoy memories and new stories. On the way out, we bump into Jamie Cromwell coming into the restaurant. And yes, this is the same now world-famous movie star, James Cromwell. How does this happen?

Don't you have stories like these? Chance events that are long shots? The good thing about them is that you know the stories are true, because they are yours or belong to someone you trust. Another interpretation that is much more confronting, questionable and inexplicable currently is that we are responsible for, and have the power to cause, these 'accidents.' We just don't yet have the scientific knowledge to explain 'how' we cause them. We do notice that coincidences happen more frequently after we experience some trauma (like divorce or death) and when we are more open emotionally to less likely, less common occurrences.

My friend Craig separated from his wife and began having a slew of coincidences. He was driving back to his Connecticut home from a speech in Massachusetts. In the car, he receives a mass email from his company's president saying that it is the first time in many years that the firm has not been included in the *Fortune Magazine* list of the top 100 companies to work for. Craig decides to go to a local restaurant to eat dinner at the bar, and happens to sit next to a woman visiting the area to consider buying a weekend place. Before long, she discloses that she is an editor at *Fortune* who among other assignments compiles an annual list of the top 100 companies to work for in America.

I met a woman who lived in Japan many years ago and was now living in Manhattan. A broker took her to look at a Connecticut house for sale. The owner of the home came outside. It happened to be her neighbor from when she lived in Japan whom she had not seen in over 15 years. She and her husband bought that house.

How does this happen?

Carl Jung thought we each have the ability to notice these supposedly random 'accidents' and even coined the term 'synchronicity' to help categorize them. He described this as meaningful coincidence. One time he was listening to a patient talk about her dream involving a gold Egyptian scarab (a jewelry ornament shaped like a beetle), and during this therapy session, there was a tapping at Jung's window. He opened it up, and in flew a type of green-gold scarab beetle.

In Arthur Koestler's 1972 book, *The Roots of Coincidence*, he suggests that quantum physics might have some answers. In that subatomic world it may be possible for time to move backward. Retro-causation, seeing the effect before the cause, could explain how some people see or influence the future before it happens. It is hard to imagine this happening, because it is so beyond our everyday experience. But people in the Middle Ages couldn't grasp that the world was rotating at 1,000 miles per hour at the equator or that the earth was not flat.

Why does any of this matter? Because it suggests that there may be ways to function in the world that aren't as obvious as what we are taught in school and learn in science textbooks. I always say now that you don't have to believe in something to pretend that it might be true.

One fall day, when my marriage was failing, I woke up and unexpectedly pictured myself spending New Year's Eve with the girl I'd taken to my senior prom. I hadn't spoken to Kay in 17 years. When I visited my father in Florida for the Christmas holidays, I called Kay and she answered. We ended up celebrating the arrival of that new year together. I was so certain that my holiday fantasy in New York would materialize.

How can that be?

In *Slaughterhouse Five*, the author Kurt Vonnegut suggests that all time has happened and is fixed, like a long tunnel through space, and his hero, Billy Pilgrim can just travel forward and backward along the path. We don't have any trouble accepting that the past is fixed, the present is instantaneous, but we all presume that the future is totally unknown. What if Vonnegut was right, and one can somehow glimpse that future that already exists, while we are just at an earlier position on the timeline?

I am not saying I believe it, but precognition dreams and moments are not that uncommon. Something is going on here. Maybe we will never know for sure.

My friend Craig told me he was driving one Sunday and had a flash of insight: he was going to do some business with Jane X, a famous weekender from New York, whom he'd never met or talked to before. Monday, he walks in his office and tells his assistant and within 15 seconds, Jane's office calls him. This has happened another time for Craig, where he thinks of someone who calls him later. Telepathy? In his case, it sometimes leads to business success. Like the time he thought of a banker he hadn't spoken to in years, and then the banker called him to arrange a mortgage. Craig is obviously very tuned in to these coincidences, which he says occur mainly during periods when he is meditating.

One day Craig is driving to the train station in New York and accidentally misses his turn. He goes to the next station and starts talking to a man on the platform who is waiting for his niece. The stranger teaches yoga in the Deep South, and is a guest teacher at his niece's yoga class in New York. When the niece arrives, she is a woman Craig knew from the Connecticut middle school his kids attend.

As strange as all this is, just consider unconventional perceptions of how the world works. When you are in your normal, unthinking routines, you might miss some cues to more productive behavior. That is what I did for years, until I had the trauma of divorce. Then I read many books to understand better what might be occurring.

There are many people who think about these interests. Astronaut Edgar Mitchell, the sixth man to walk on the moon, explored consciousness and paranormal phenomena. On Mitchell's way back to earth during the Apollo 14 flight he had a powerful savikalpa samādhi experience—a high state of bliss, spiritual consciousness and union with the universe. Mitchell also claimed to have conducted private ESP (extrasensory perception) experiments with his friends on Earth. The results of these experiments were published in the Journal of Parapsychology in 1971. He is the founder of the Institute of Noetic Sciences (IONS) for the purpose of consciousness research and other "related phenomena."

I went to IONS in California and subscribed to its magazine for a while. But I still haven't come to any firm conclusions. Sometimes, I think all humans and objects are connected somehow–there is a hologram theory–and some of us can read these clues better than others. Maybe you just need to learn how to do it, like reading letters and words.

No matter, I mention all these stories in hopes that you will open your minds to the best technique of all for making easy decisions in all aspects of your lives: developing your intuition. I have trained myself how to do it and have read how others, especially some hugely successful businessmen, have used their powers of intuition to wend their way through their lives. So much of what we do is determined by the choices we make: career, marriage, investment, travel, children.

Let me tell you about intuition and hunches, and how I learned to trust them. I have made a lot of money by trusting my intuition.

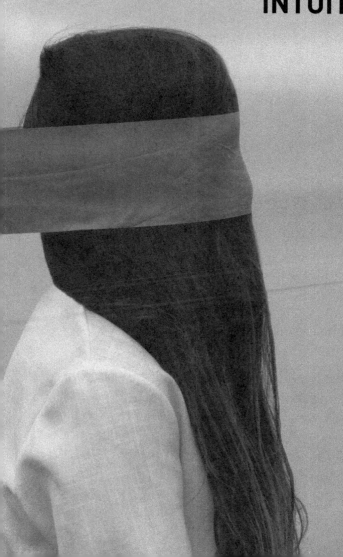

CHAPTER FIFTEEN

INTUITION

I was separated and living alone in Manhattan in the late 70s. One day, after a business meeting 17 blocks from my office, I had this insane urge to not hail a cab, but to start running up Madison Avenue, in my suit and with my attaché case. It sounds crazy, but I dashed off until I reached 53rd Street, on the northeast corner, when I felt I had to stop. Within seconds a bus pulled up, and out stepped a woman whom I'd known in college and had not seen or thought about for maybe 14 years.

"Flipchick!" I yelled, recalling her strange nickname. We spoke for a few minutes, and she was nice enough to give me the phone number of Alice, her close friend from college, a girl I had liked at the time. I called Alice, and we dated for nine months.

How do I explain that mad urge to sprint up the street in a suit? I had my share of coincidentally finding parking spaces and bumping into people I knew as I walked down the street. But that was weird.

However, I would say that my biggest successes, in my post-divorce life, have all resulted from learning how to recognize, trust and act on my intuitions. Even if they tell me to start running uptown at rush hour. I use a simple three-statement motto for making everyday or even major, consequential decisions: If it feels right, do it. If it feels wrong, don't do it. If you are not sure, don't do it.

Whether you are considering purchasing a shirt or a car, asking someone out, making an investment, or business choice. This strategy can probably be used to help make almost any decision, whether it's to apply for a job, choose a career field, decide what to eat in a restaurant.

In fact, those simple, barely significant decisions like food and movie choices are the perfect times to practice for the big ones, like buying a house or investing in your first business.

The hardest part is to avoid doing the safe or easy thing that people expect or tell you that you should do. We are so conditioned to be cool and in control or macho or logical. But hearing, listening to and acting on intuitions and hunches is a complete departure from all those "should do's." It took me lots of practice to even glimpse or notice in my brain that there was another path or course of action I was being prompted to consider. It took a good bit of courage to deviate from the obvious and predictable choices I had been taught to make.

What exactly IS an intuition? One dictionary defines it as, "a direct perception of truth, fact, etc., independent of any reasoning process; immediate apprehension." Another as, "the ability to understand something immediately, without the need for conscious reasoning."

Hopefully, you can relate to this experience. I know there are people who wonder if they have ever been in love? They are just not sure, even though they have lived for decades. I don't presume that everyone has intuitions.

It doesn't matter. Just remember that three-statement motto, and you are on your way to making better decisions that will help you create better life. I define that as being a positive, uplifting, sometimes joyful way of being that brings you closer to your four major goals for: good health, wealth, happiness and wisdom. These topics are the most common subjects that a freelance journalist should write about to sell articles for money; that's because people are intensely interested in knowing about these issues.

While you can't summarize decision-making and people's lives so simplistically, it's a start. You can always complicate it with greater depth and intellectual sophistication, but most of us are not that intense, so start simple.

Let me tell you some major ways that my life was changed by my trusting my intuition and ignoring logic.

When I finished my two years in the army, at age 23, I had to take whatever job I could find. That job was a production editor's job at Prentice Hall publishing company for $85 a week. I'd written some reports in the army and liked the writing process. After two months, I was ready to quit, because the job involved zero writing. I was just involved in the manufacture of textbooks, but my father urged me to stick it out until my five months' review.

Three months later, my boss told me with great pride that I was receiving a huge 10% raise of $8.00 a week before withholdings.

I told him immediately, "I quit!"

He said I shouldn't do that, because it was a big company, there were lots of opportunities, and "just this week the president asked if there was anyone to fill the director's slot in the public relations department." Seems the former director had quit after eight years in the position.

Without hesitancy, I asked, "Did you mention my name?" "No, I didn't know you had any interest in that," he said.

"I do," I told him.

That night I asked my wife who worked in an ad agency, "What's public relations? Is it when you have a man in a gorilla suit climb the Empire State Building to promote the movie King Kong?"

After two to three weeks of tests of my writing skills, while reading how to write PR copy and what the field was all about, I was not hired to be the PR Director. The head of book publicity had that responsibility added to his job as well. I was to be a swing assistant to the two assistant directors of both the Public Relations and Book Publicity departments.

However, one week after I started, the Assistant PR Director gave one day's notice and left. I was instructed to take over running the entire department, under the supervision of the Book Publicity Director, who was overloaded with all his previous commitments.

It was just me and Thelma the secretary. I had already signed up for a night course in Public Relations at the New School in New York. I began to learn on the job how to write articles, hire photographers for annual report and house magazine photos, set up meetings, meet editors as I promoted the company's wall street requirements and tax advice services, etc. These skills helped me to start my own book publishing company 10 years later.

I was lucky that I spoke up so unhesitatingly in that meeting. I did that even though I had no idea what I was doing. That is how intuition works. It's not reasonable, logical or makes any sense at all. I could never have predicted that if I waited three more months that exact job that had been filled for eight years would suddenly became vacant. These kinds of events seem to happen all the time, when you trust your intuitive side.

The first time I met my present wife, I was there to sell her advertising space in my books. We had a couple of business lunches. I was intensely attracted to her. Our developing relationship was put on hold for a few weeks, when I went to the USSR to participate in a book project. I was there to help coordinate a pictorial view of the entire country taken during 24 hours by 100 photographers.

My future wife and I reconnected in Spain. We were falling madly in love. None of it made sense: I had been trying to find a significant other for years, and here I was ready to commit to one after just three dates. Her husband had died just a few months earlier after a long illness, so I suspected that I was the rebound guy. But being with her seemed so right, so real and deep. We instantly became a committed couple. It was truly love at first—or third—sight. That had never happened to me before. I had been single for 12 years and dated lots of women. I believed that if this new relationship fell apart after a few months, I will have at least enjoyed those months.

But it never ended. We moved in together right away, married a year later, raised two kids, started or invested in maybe a dozen private companies, and it's now 32 years since that first business lunch at the Union Square Café in Manhattan. Against all odds, despite any logic of how crazy it seemed, contrary to common sense and the likelihood that this connection was simply a fling, it has worked. My gut said it was right. I went with it even though I had my usual rational doubts. But my intuition was on target, and it made the decision to commit and marry no decision at all.

Some intuitive decisions seem easier, like giving up my nightly ice cream treat after discovering at a routine annual physical that my cholesterol level had spiked to near-heart-attack range. Done in a flash.

Deciding whether to close on our present house was much harder, because between contract signing and day of deed transfer and 90% balance of money exchange, 9/11 happened. Should we walk away from our down payment? Not take on the increased responsibility? Somehow it felt "right" to proceed with the purchase. No regrets since. Another good choice.

An out-of-town friend stopped by an hour after calling and invited me to join him on a scientific expedition to Mongolia. Crazy. That country wasn't on my bucket list. But I knew in an instant that I was going to be there. Just intuitive. Quick decisions. Followed up by some rational justification over the next few days.

Haven't you felt that certainty about some choices you had to make even if it didn't make any sense at all? I presume most of them worked out okay. Wouldn't you like more decisions to be that simple?

Train yourself to bring out that intuitive side of yourself with the little daily decisions. Then you might be able to apply that skill to the life-changing, much bigger choices. Especially the ones involving money and career.

CHAPTER SIXTEEN

PERSONAL RELATIONSHIPS

For the first four years of my life, during World War II, my father was away in the Coast Guard, so I was raised by three women: my working-at-a-job mother, her sister Rose and an African American babysitter/cleaning lady. I suspect this early upbringing led me to be more comfortable with females. They talked a lot, expressed emotions and feelings, and focused on personal issues, just like I do now.

I've also decided that if most 'normal' men's genes and inclinations are 85% male and 15% female in their stereotypical behaviors, I am about 75% male and 25% female. For years, I minded that most men I met talked little about themselves. Their conversations focused on sports, government and political events and careers/business. I found it very limiting and often boring. I like getting deeper into personality issues, the why and what of our decisions, actions, morals.

One result is that my relationships with girlfriends and wives seemed very different from many of my male friends and acquaintances. I think I have a better sense than some of what it takes to make someone else happy. I can see things from the other person's point of view. I am willing to give in or compromise, without feeling my ego has suffered. Lots of men just can't do this.

Now relationships with romantic partners are the ones that poets, songwriters and filmmakers write about. These are the relationships that are the most demanding. But there are many other interactions that demand our attention as well: parents, children, bosses, employees, friends and acquaintances, strangers, customers. The list is pretty long.

You may have to deal with large egos; people who think

the world should revolve around them and treat others as if they exist only to serve their needs and wants. This works for infants who need to cry to receive food and warmth. However, many adults are still functioning in that mode. I see it around me all the time, and it's not a good way to engage people.

My daughter's first word was, "Mine." She knew her older brother was taking her toys and fought back. For the next 15 or so years, Skylar wouldn't share food at the dinner table with anyone. Her food was hers. When she wanted a taste of the meal I'd ordered in a restaurant, she was always surprised that I would let her have some. Now that she is in her 20s, she is happy to share. She has learned that being selfish is not the best way to have friends and caring relationships. There are many adults who can't do that. They don't share, they aren't considerate—it is still all about them.

I often tell people one of the best-kept secrets to my happy marriage is that I do the dishes. My wife prepares the food; I clean up the kitchen. She also works. Why shouldn't we divide some of the household responsibilities? I prepare the taxes and deal with the cars. She oversees the housecleaning and much of the kids' school interactions. I know men who disagree. The wife runs the house, all the kids' stuff, all the kitchen stuff. Even if the wife has an outside job too. After dinner, many men head straight for the TV and the sports game. Washing dishes is women's work. How is your wife supposed to love you and want to make you happy and have sex with you if you are the only one who counts?

I knew a man who didn't want his wife to work, even though she wanted to. "A woman's place is in the home," and this husband's friends would make fun of him for not controlling his wife or making enough money for the two of them. That marriage ended within a few years unsurprisingly.

The demands some men I know have made on their wives can be surprising. One insists that certain foods in the refrigerator always be in the same place on the same shelf, so he knows instantly where to find them, and doesn't have to waste time looking. He insists that his life be very efficient. But what does this do to his wife's view of their relationship? Where is the give and take?

Reminds me of a former boss who bragged that he saved time by dictating, while he was on the toilet. Now that's efficient. But I met that man's wife after two years of being one of only two junior executives who worked for him: she'd never heard of me. Unbelievable to me. What else don't they tell each other?

You need to talk to people. They can't read your mind. My mother liked to make fun of my father after they divorced, because she once told him that she was cold as they were walking. "He told me to take deep breaths," she would relate in a ridiculing tone, "when I wanted him to put his arms around me." But she never understood that you must tell people what you want or like. Especially about love and sex, but also about a million other situations.

It's not easy. People are messy. We are all insecure. We all bluff and lie or withhold the full story. Maybe that works with strangers or occasional business deals. But it's a terrible strategy with your mate or people you will continue to be in contact with.

That is why so many people are in bad relationships. Marriages that are disappointing, adult children who won't talk to their parents, employees who hate their bosses. We all put up with what we feel are injustices and egos to make a living. Economics is super important. But that aside, can you imagine how much better some situations would be if you spoke up to the person dominating you?

More than half of all marriages in America end up in divorce. Mine did as well, though it took 10 years. We just changed in our interests and desires for how to live a life. Some of my friends thought I was brave at the time. I thought it was essential. But then after that rupture, I had a better idea of what I wanted/needed in a partner. I think I learned from my experience.

My second marriage, 12 years later, has now been going for 32 years. My role models were Charles and Ray Eames, two designers of buildings, furniture (Eames chair) and movies who worked together full time. My knowledge of their happiness level is zilch. But my superficial view of their daily togetherness seemed ideal.

I am not suggesting that you should also search as I did for a wife employed in your field or who can join you in business projects. But I am encouraging you to think about what works for you. When I was dating, I would turn down any blind date with a woman who smoked. I didn't smoke and didn't like to be around smokers. Simple. But many people get married thinking they can change their loved one's habits and values. That is a very steep uphill climb that can cause arguments and lead to emotional distance or divorce.

Giving in and understanding differences makes it easier to deal with people. Accepting that the other person has a view that is not the same as yours helps to facilitate conversation and compassion so we can meet in the middle. Common ground. These days in partisan politics, compromising is surrendering. The mantra preaches that one should never give an inch from the pure position that one knows is right. If you are a politician who needs to win re-election in a gerrymandered district, it's easy to understand why you are so principled publicly. Even if you are secretly a huge hypocrite. But in normal society, not seeing both sides or not compromising doesn't always work. You want to sell your house, you better be willing to come off your asking price, so the buyer can feel she has made a good deal. You want to convince your employees to work harder? You better motivate them partly by giving them some perks and rewards for outstanding performance. People thrive when they are appreciated. Obvious, right?

It isn't to everyone. When I am in Japan and chat with the waiters, my friends there point out that servers are used to being ignored and barely acknowledged. That is their custom, and I have trouble adopting it. Maybe my friendliness makes them uncomfortable. Though, I don't think so.

In most countries, it's not socially acceptable to act rude in shops and restaurants. But the customer is always right, and the employees better bite their tongues and smile. Typically, people who are rude in one setting carry that behavior into all their relationships. What does that do to those relationships? They are not harmonious. Maybe Mr. Rude guy can buy his way everywhere or has power in other ways. He may be totally insensitive. He may not care about what people think of him. But that isn't the kind of relationship you want to be in, is it?

I don't think it works to be a despot, unless you are taking over countries or buying businesses. Then you must be tough, but that is a different playing field.

My father made me read a Dale Carnegie self-help book called, *How to Win Friends and Influence People*. It's so simple to grasp some basic concepts about getting along with others, some simple ideas like: pronounce their names correctly, listen instead of talking all the time, ask people questions, instead of always telling them your stories.

I've mentioned my success in using aikido's martial art techniques to throw people off balance in business and many other areas. It's so easy, predictable and works so astonishingly well in everyday, non-physical relationships.

Do you recall, when I printed a customer's picture in my book and he hated the quality of the color? I let him rant and scream, and I was kind and respectful. He was so surprised when I agreed with him and gave him what he wanted. He apologized. He was ashamed for being so abusive. We worked out a discount on his bill. This client told others what a good publisher I was, and he became a repeat advertiser.

I built a successful business with a startling gimmick: I told the truth. Honesty is so rare in the money-grubbing, commercial world that I amazed people all the time. They were satisfied and eager and happy to keep working with me. It was astonishing to me. I created a thriving enterprise that generated revenues of a few million dollars a year by offering a decent service and telling the truth. By recognizing that how I saw things did not matter to the people paying me. What mattered was how they viewed what I was providing them. And I learned real fast to compromise.

Personal relationships work the same way, I believe. It is an exchange, there are different degrees of influence and power held by the opposing parties. But if you "win" all the time by squeezing and crushing your spouse or your friend or your child, it will eventually stop working.

If it always needs to be your way, then the other person can't be happy. And that will affect how your partner views the relationship and treats you when you are together. Isn't it obvious? How can you tell your wife she uses too much toilet paper and expect her to be comfortable when you are home judging her every move?

You must be considerate. You need to talk about what you want. And I know that is difficult. It's all about finding what works for you. There is no right or wrong. I have encountered many kinds of relationships. I have met many people who can't understand why their relationships are so frustrating.

In 1936, Benny Goodman recorded a song called *The Glory of Love* that I heard in the 50s, when the Five Keys also made it a best seller. It's also been covered by Paul McCartney and Bette Midler. Some of the lyrics just came to me regarding relationships:

You have to, "win a little, lose a little...give a little, take a little."

Cynics will say this is very simplistic, but look around from now on, and notice how few people can do this comfortably. However, if you are willing to give in to the other person's ideas, you will see how much better your life can be.

CHAPTER SEVENTEEN

UNDERSTANDING OTHER PEOPLE'S NEED TO BE SUPERIOR

In the 1990s, when we were breeding Shetland ponies—we had 70 at one point and dropped 20 babies a year—there was a mare we bought named 104. When she was the newest member of the herd, she was not allowed by the others to come in the barn; another mare guarded the door. Poor 104 would have to stand outside shivering in the rain and mud or the snow and the cold.

We felt so sorry for her, but that is how the hierarchy of herds works. The ponies, like other animal groups, create a pecking order, a way of relating to each other, so that one has more power or perks than those ranked lower. It's how their society functions. We left them to their normal behavior.

Eventually, a pony from the herd died or was sold, and 104 was allowed in the barn. She moved up to be the guard at the barn door. Can you guess what happened? She had zero empathy. She wouldn't let newer ponies inside. She was heartless. I have no right to impose human values on her, like remembering how miserable she'd been outside in the rain and having some pity on the ponies she was keeping outside now herself. Still, it seemed so mean.

After observing animal practices like these, I noticed that humans were behaving similarly. Regardless of whether they were sophisticated heads of state, intelligent academics, businessmen, housewives or uneducated laborers. They were constantly ranking themselves. All economic classes. No matter how respected or successful. It was pathetic. I decided that humans are just animals, and they can't help themselves.

It's useful to understand what I think is going on.

To begin with, most people are herd animals; nothing derogatory intended here. Groups of folks have a better chance of fighting off the enemy tribe, so all kinds of customs and rules and acceptable behaviors evolve in the community. Perfectly natural. With familiarity comes a distrust of different patterns: my tribe's/country's/culture's/religion's way is how one should behave.

This world view exists everywhere today. It leads to all kinds of groups being formed, and all kinds of group members believing or wanting their group to rank higher or be superior. In case there is no proof or definitive agreement about who's "better," a simple solution is to put down other groups or their members, because that then elevates you and your group.

While ridiculous, it's pervasive.

I wrote earlier about how almost all people need to be part of a group and that groups go to extraordinary efforts to convince their members and other groups that they are superior.

Think about how some northerners (in the US) believe they work harder and are also superior to southerners. How many Germans think they are more efficient than those living near the Mediterranean. People from sunny Italy, Spain and Greece are often judged to be more relaxed and less uptight than the rigid, more subdued folks from the gray, rainy, snowy northern countries.

Look at the hostility during World Cup soccer contests and Davis Cup matches, where residents identify with their national teams and sometimes are so angry that riots and deaths break out.

Think of all the wars that have occurred, because of a president or emperor wanting to have more territory, gold or power than the head of another country. Recollect how gentiles sometimes didn't want Jews in their neighborhood or club. There are whites who said the same about blacks.

The list is incredibly long. And it controls or greatly influences our actions and values. People will do almost anything to make themselves superior.

Some of this need to be on top results from envy and jealousy. It's one thing to want the success, intelligence, good fortune, money (all envy), and it's another to resent another's having these benefits (jealous). But I think it's simply human nature. We are probably built this way to spur our species to survive.

We all want the good things in life, whether through our own efforts or by taking away someone else's achievements or gifts. And if we can't acquire them, then many of us help ourselves feel better by acting superior or putting the more successful person down. We can all think of examples where people have intentionally hurt someone just to inflate their own egos or rationalize their limitations:

My house was used to host a fundraiser. A guest at the event was married to the head of the local garden club. This person said that my wife shouldn't get credit for her beautiful gardens, because she used an outside gardener and didn't do all the work herself. The speaker was clearly trying to make his spouse feel better by putting my wife down.

I was at a dinner party, sitting next to a man who told me that his company was just completing an acquisition of a company that would bring all the revenues under his control to $1 billion. He tried several times to let me know that he was more important than I was. All that money and power and success, and he still had to boast to a stranger.

The ironic thing was that he was written up in the paper a few years later for owing the most back taxes of anyone in town, his wife left him, the bank took over his house, and he went to federal prison for bankruptcy fraud and tax evasion.

After we moved to the country from NY City, some of our friends felt that we were rejecting their values. When one visited the loft we still owned in the city, she had the audacity to say right to our faces that "my street is better than your street." This is a grown, respected professional in her 40s. But she still had to elevate herself by acting like a child and putting us down. This behavior is not something that only children display. Grownups do it, too.

Misunderstanding these concepts can be confusing. A distant relative of mine once whined to me that he was very attracted to a young woman, but that woman spurned him and chose someone else. He had an astonishing view of how the world worked: "My car is better than that guy's car. How could she choose him over me?"

I once dated a woman who couldn't cook very well. She was annoyed that I wasn't a good cook. When she hosted one important dinner party with friends she wanted to impress, she hired the owner of a nearby restaurant to bring in the food and then told her guests that she had cooked the food herself. This woman was an author, speaker, and very respected personage. Yet she still had to lie to puff herself up even more. That relationship didn't last for me.

In the late 60s, when I was doing financial public relations, I arranged for *Forbes* magazine to interview my client. When he was 22, this entrepreneur had borrowed $25,000 from his father for a unique business idea he came up with in college. By the age of 29, he was worth $50 million. As my client told his story, the reporter blurted out: "Well I beat you in one way, I have four kids, which is more than you!"

In the next decades, this brilliant businessman did everything he could to acquire more wealth and power than Donald Trump. He was the youngest person under 30 to acquire that amount of wealth on his own. But it wasn't enough. He had to beat the Donald. He even said, "I'll own the world. I could even be the first Jewish president."

I heard he was worth $800 million at one point, before his empire collapsed into bankruptcy, and he was forced to sell his art, apartment, and businesses.

To be accepted in high-status groups, people will do almost anything. Jack Grubman earned $20 million a year as Wall Street's highest ever paid security analyst. That was until he fraudulently upgraded AT&T, so that his two-year-old twins could be accepted into a kiddie program at an exclusive New York City private school.

What was the connection? Mr. X, a top executive of a major bank who was also on the board of AT&T, persuaded the school's admissions department by arranging for a $1 million donation from the bank's foundation. When it all came out—along with other deeds—Jack was fined $15 million and barred for life from the securities industry. He was one of the few Wall Streeters caught and punished for their bad behavior. But these two rich and powerful men were willing to risk their careers and reputations for even more money and superiority. Seems pretty dumb, doesn't it?

When I applied to a country club with nearby tennis courts, I was told during the interview that I was surely a weekender from New York, because the only people in Connecticut who had beards were tradesmen like plumbers and carpenters. Where do people come up with these ideas? What a provincial. Took some will power not to ridicule him in front of the other club members. I was accepted anyway, but only played tennis there one summer.

Don't get me wrong, people want to be comfortable with other people. Especially, if members are considering allowing someone into their group. Perfectly reasonable. That woman who lied about her cooking also urged me to wear more conventional clothing, because clothes are a signal that you are good enough to be accepted. That's why there are fashion styles to signal that you are a hipster in boots and black for Brooklyn. Or maybe well off enough to buy a $200 Hermes tie, or a $500 Burberry scarf suitable for, and expected at, the private club on the Upper East Side of Manhattan.

When I first came to my small rural town, I learned that casual did not mean slacks and a shirt, it meant a sport jacket and tie, rather than a suit. I wanted to be accepted, so I wore the jacket (but not the tie) and didn't have any problem doing so.

Years earlier I discovered that the difference in men's suits between a $300 one off the rack and a $2000 one custom made might include details like button holes: the former sewn by machine and the latter by hand. Naturally the fit was better, as was the cloth. But I didn't have $2000 for a suit, so I made do and rationalized. Maybe men owning hand-sewn button holes noticed this distinction and felt superior to those of us in the ready-made garment.

I eventually started a publishing company that worked with photographers who all wore jeans and sneakers. Me too. I was much more comfortable in that costume. I had an office where my partner owned a photography gallery on Fifth Avenue and 57th Street, directly across from Tiffany's. One year my father visited from Miami, tootled around the office, and told me I was doing it all wrong: "You should be wearing a suit! Look more respectable, like a professional."

Ha! My clients would never have trusted me in such an outfit. You need to know your audience. But he was certain that I wasn't doing things the correct way, because as a doctor, he always wore a suit or sport jacket and tie. He knew what worked for him so he assumed it was also right for me. People need to feel superior, and one way to reach that height is to tell others the "correct" way to behave. Incidentally, at that point I was making in one year about 40-50 times what he was earning. But I never told him.

Another relative had such a minimal business that his parents subsidized him almost every year they were alive. He would often boast to me that revenues were up 30% and try to impress me with his meager sales. My company was doing 60-70 times more than his.

One year he visited our farm and proudly showed me his daily planner, a real fad at that time. It was a 6X9 hard back binder with loose leaf pages for every day and hour of the year. It allowed him to organize his life. In fact, I had been very impressed that he called me nine months in advance to tell me the exact hour and minute that he was going to arrive. A few months later, he called to shift the arrival time by 45 minutes. Incredible.

After he came and was toured around the farm, with its 240 acres, 150 animals, farm manager, three barns and two houses, he confronted me with a very troubled reaction: "You need a day book," he informed me. "You can't function without it." He said I needed it to be a success. He went on and on about how improved my life would be, once I started using it.

This time I did speak up, after all, he was "family." "Hey, look around. Can't you see that I am doing pretty well without it?" was the essence of my retort. But if he could see my reality, he couldn't admit it. He knew better, he was smarter, he understood success better than I do: I needed to use a day planner.

It's all maddening, this constant bumping into other people's ideas of how one should behave, what one must do, how one must dress, talk, think, where you need to live, which is the only hotel to stay at on vacation, what to eat. Good god. One friend insists that I can't eat anything but vegetables... and no eggs or dairy either. Otherwise I will be sick and miserable all the time. I stopped going out to meals with her, because every choice I made was so toxic she couldn't stand it and had to tell me how I was killing myself with every bite.

People feel the need to always be right and convince themselves that what they are doing is better and best. It makes them feel superior and gives them some false assurance that they are living life correctly. Why can't they just live and let live?

If you understand this universal attribute to be superior and can deal with it without fighting back all the time, you are probably a guru or a saint. There is nothing rational about it. However, if you want to be admitted to their club, then you may have to wear a suit, shave your beard, and not use profanity. Learn to talk about sports or business, leer at women, drink a lot. Maybe you have to be willing to smoke dope or snort cocaine, eat like a horse or pretend you have a good marriage and perfect kids.

These choices will determine your success with some groups of people. It's a very difficult and often pothole-filled road. Choose a hippy colony and you may have to smoke pot and share your wife. Choose an artist colony and you may have to conceal that your family has money. It's not easy to get along with others. We are all individuals with unique talents, looks, varying budgets and bank accounts, preferences and histories.

Most of us want to be appreciated and applauded, recognized more than the next person. Rewarded for our efforts and given medals and prizes for our achievements. There are whole cultures and industries granting Nobels and Pulitzers, Oscars, Emmys, Clios and Tonys. The local garden club has awards, so do school sports leagues, so do religious organizations that celebrate leaders in different industries to help raise funds at recognition dinners.

Don't you want to stand out and be cheered? Wouldn't it be special to be one of the few whose play was produced? Book was published? New business went public?

We want more money to have comforts and calm. We may also want our name on a building or a google website. We want to have children we can be proud of, and the mother who doesn't embarrass us, and the husband who doesn't drink too much. But we are lion cubs scrapping in the jungle. We want mama to like us best. We want to be stronger and smarter and tougher than the others. We want to have no serious health issues. All these goals and wants are what we strive for. To be in a good group that people respect, admire and wish they could be part of.

It's a challenge. But now you are armed with the knowledge that the higher you rise, the more people will attempt to tear you down. It's a fight and a battle. I hope you have the stomach for it. Remember, you can always drop out, find your private oasis, and live happily ever after.

CHAPTER EIGHTEEN

HEALTH

When I was young, I had a short list of values that I had prioritized in the following order:

Wisdom > Happiness > Health > Wealth

When I was in the army, I contracted hepatitis and jaundice in Korea. I had volunteered to be the liaison officer for the country's largest orphanage, where I ate food that was fertilized with human waste. The whites of my eyes turned brown, as did my urine. I was flown on a stretcher to hospitals in Japan and Washington, DC. I was weary, exhausted. It took me weeks to be able to walk just one city block. After that event, I reordered my list of what is important:

Health > Wealth > Wisdom> Happiness

Over the next 50 years, health has never left the top. It has retained first place. Without it, I don't believe you can concentrate on the other three goals and activities. Especially earning money, doing your job, adapting to economic changes. Certainly, happiness is a lot easier to attain if you are not sick or weak or having trouble walking. Yet so many people I see and read about seem indifferent to their health. Maybe they've never been seriously ill, so they take wellness for granted. But they must know or hear about people who have been sick or hospitalized.

My father was a chiropractor who would often say to me, "You are what you eat." He also told me that to avoid overeating, "It's better in the garbage can than in your stomach." He showed me how to live a healthy life. Many people thought my dad to be somewhat of a "quack" in the 1950s for accepting chiropractic's contributions to healing, but he walked the talk, when it came to healthy living. He was hardly ever sick enough to not go to work. I can only remember two times he was ailing during my entire childhood. He watched most of his friends suffer illnesses he never had, and they died ahead of him too. I also heard about his patients who didn't take care of themselves, ignored his suggestions and paid the price uncomfortably.

With this upbringing, I had some idea of what was good and bad to eat. I knew there was a direct correlation between what you ate and how you felt. I was shown pictures of the effects of alcoholism on the pores of your nose. I probably figured out that drinking and driving was a risky business as well. It's all so logical. It's basic cause and effect. But what was drummed into me that my peers probably didn't hear is that the results of poor diet, smoking and a lack of exercise don't show up right away. The consequences of unhealthy living will typically surface after 20 to 30 years.

No matter what I knew or not, my first day away at college, I was pigging out at McDonalds. I recognized that I was ignoring dad's principles. And, over the years and decades, I came around to a healthy life.

Somehow I have the discipline to deny myself food that is bad for me, even though I love it. I avoided junk food early on, and gave up meat (not fish and fowl) in my 30s. I love cheeses, desserts, cream sauces, butter. Who doesn't? For years, I ate ice cream with chocolate syrup almost every night. But when suddenly after decades of annual physicals, my cholesterol spiked into the near heart attack range, I immediately learned what cholesterol was—who knew? I learned what foods caused it or contained it, then modified my diet and saw those high numbers disappear. That's who I am.

Others take a statin pill, so they don't have to change

anything. A few say that life without all those delicious foods isn't worth living, and if they die a few years sooner because of unhealthy food, smoking or couch-sitting, who cares. Pick your poison.

Some just don't realize what is going on. One friend, for example, complained of having gained 30 pounds inexplicably, as he drank almost a whole bottle of wine with his take-out pizza meal and then had an entire bar of dark Belgian chocolate. How could he not see the connection? Eating healthy is about making the right choices, not necessarily the choices we want to make. Unfortunately, some friends have complained that they resent my presence at their table, when I pass on certain foods, because it makes them feel guilty for indulging themselves.

Everyone wants to live a long time. However, not with strokes from poor diet that incapacitate you in your 50s or 60s. I know people like that. They've made it to older age, but their day-to-day is horribly limited. Some are in wheelchairs for 20 years. Is it worth it to have eaten all that fattening, non-nutritious food? I am not referring to people who are big genetically. Or who are impaired from accidents or illnesses. But I am thinking of many contemporaries in their 70s who are so large from overeating that they can't walk effortlessly and need canes or walkers. Sadly they are part of those statistics that declare one third of Americans as obese and a second third as overweight. And with this heaviness come numerous diseases and ailments. Such a shame, because so many harmful habits and activities could have been altered, if there had been the awareness and the will to change destructive behavior.

Being conscious of your strengths and weaknesses is

obviously crucial, when you are choosing a career. It's clear early on what your individual talents and capabilities are. I could see in high school that I was not skilled as a painter or musician. I didn't like the idea of being a doctor around sick people or want to spend my time indoors as an accountant. I had to assess my proficiencies and then enter a field where I excelled or had serious interest, even if I made false starts in college and afterwards.

The same self-evaluation should be applied to your body and health too. Tennis great Novak Djokovic was collapsing in matches, had trouble breathing, and was vomiting during toilet breaks. He discovered that his body needed to avoid gluten. Within 12 months after changing his diet,[20] he had so much more energy and stamina that his game improved dramatically, and he became number one in the world.

For decades, my daughter had headaches and indigestion after eating. She tried different diets that changed nothing. Then she switched to a high fat, low carbohydrate menu, and the headaches and stomach aches stopped happening. It's not quite a miracle, but it certainly demonstrates that getting to know your own body's preferences and responses is a very big deal.

In my world, nothing is more important than good health. After I learned in 2005 that I had the cholesterol problem, I was devastated. All that dairy fat I'd been enjoying for years was having a life-threatening effect. Though I was told that I could simply take statins, I decided to try diet and heavy exercise first. I eliminated almost all the high cholesterol foods. For a few weeks, I rowed aggressively on a machine every day. My cholesterol dropped substantially. I toned down the exercise, kept the same diet, and I was fine for 10 years.

Then I learned after my 2015 annual checkup that to maintain optimum fitness, I needed to start statins. I accepted that guidance from three cardiologists and continue to exercise moderately and avoid fatty foods.

Of course, everyone is unique. I meet plenty of people who stay thin and have no cholesterol issues, no matter what or how much they eat: their metabolism is different from those who seem to gain weight from lettuce leaves. You must identify how your body works and respect its proclivities.

But then we change—or our environment changes—so you have to stay alert and keep monitoring that individual body of yours. After I moved up north from Florida for college and encountered the seasons for the first time, I discovered only then that I am allergic to ragweed in the fall and pollen in the spring. I knew a woman who raised and boarded horses for decades, until one day she discovered that she was suddenly allergic to horses, and had a potentially fatal reaction.

When most people learn that their life is in danger from food or something else in their surroundings, they often act smartly and accept some change. But there are many people who are addicted to alcohol and drugs or who smoke tobacco or drink coffee for the jolt of caffeine who know about the negative intakes and continue ingesting them. Studies show that people can also be addicted to sugar.[21] Brain behavior on sugar is similar to what happens when you take certain drugs. There is an American cultural norm that chooses breakfast foods so full of sugar that they can be considered desserts! Yet the food corporations promote these harmful morning and kid products as if they are healthy and good for you. You might pay more attention to how much sugar you are eating. However, if you are like me, resisting sweets is a battle.

I have mentioned how hard it is to make lifestyle changes. Especially when most people don't worry about results that are 20 to 50 years away. One day on British TV, a doctor in Ibiza disclosed that one out of five Brits goes there to have sex. The doc asked visitors there if they used condoms, and none of the men said they did. The doctor asked if the men were aware of the risk of STD's and they all did, but still did not take precautions.

When I was 16 traveling to Washington, DC to march with my high school band in the Cherry Blossom Parade, we visited the Smithsonian Institution. I saw a three-foot high photo of a naked man with syphilis. There was a pockmarked, syphilitic penis in a bottle of formaldehyde. It scared the hell out of me for life. Most terrifying was reading that the bacteria inside of you often didn't blossom for decades.

Many people don't worry about the future. Very understandable. I can't say I always practiced safe sex. Then the HIV/AIDS epidemic happened. I knew people were dying of the disease. It was Russian roulette without a pistol. Yet all of us seem willing to take these chances.

I read about a famous, stunt BMX bicyclist, Mat Hoffman, whose career resulted in all kinds of broken bones and other injuries. He was driven to compete and perform new tricks that would terrify his audiences. A buddy of Mat's said Mat viewed his body as just another bike part. Mat said, "If I died with a body that wasn't completely wrecked, then I'd feel like I completely wasted it." He also said that he wakes up knowing that each day there is a good chance he will die.

Mat has had 23 surgeries. 100 concussions. 300 stitches. 2 comas. 60 broken bones. I saw a video of him doing his own suturing without anesthesia to a pedal gash on his leg, so he doesn't have to waste time going to the hospital. Like Rambo.

Most of us aren't as extreme as Mat. I can't believe that anyone wants to be sick or injured and find it difficult to walk or function without pain. Am I naive? Then why do so few pay so little heed to the obvious results of inaction.

Along with nutrition, exercise is another major ingredient of good health. The Center for Disease Control and Prevention (CDC) analyzed survey data from 450,000 American adults (18 and older) and concluded that only 21% met the US Government (Department of Health and Human Services) recommendation for weekly exercise. This included aerobic and muscle-strengthening activity. However, 52% did realize at least 2 1/2 hours per week of moderate intensity aerobic exercise (including brisk walking, lawn mowing) or 75 minutes of vigorous intensity aerobics (like running). 29% did muscle strengthening activities (like weight machines, push-ups) at least twice a week.

"Too often, Americans reach for pills to treat their ills, rather than turning to lifestyle changes that can boost their health," said Charles H. Hennekens, M.D., a professor at Florida Atlantic University's College of Medicine who co-authored a 2015 report to determine why so many Americans are obese and overweight. About 36 percent of U.S. adults do not engage in any type of exercise or leisure-time activity.

I used to be one of those inactive people. After years of office work and never having time to work out, I somehow started in my 40s to practice a Japanese martial art called aikido. Three years later I switched to a Brazilian martial art called capoeira and even went to Brazil to study for a week with members of my class, who were mostly in their 20s. I then became too busy again and stopped working out.

When I was in my mid-60s, I joined a gym and saw that some people were going three or four times a week. I had heard that there had been a fitness revolution. I learned that millions of people were exercising and playing sports after work and on weekends their entire lives. Where had I been? Totally out of touch.

"You better use it or you'll lose it," was the common reference to muscles and genitals. Decades of not stretching and using muscles leads to flabbiness, low stamina, poor lung capacity, stiffness, aches and soreness. Obvious. Yet tens of millions do nothing about it. On the other hand, there is a smaller group of gym goers, outdoor and sports lovers who are fit, hiking, and playing games like tennis into their late 80s and even 90s. Some have even worn away cartilage, and torn joints from so many years of sports that they had procedures and replacements on shoulders, knees and hips to keep playing. Now that is determination.

They don't do it for the long-term benefits of good health. They just love it, find satisfaction in the movement, competition, the eye-hand coordination challenge, the victory, the new personal best, the thrill of a rappelling descent or the view from the top of a mountain climbed. They are a special breed in our domesticated society. The fortunate few who need to be active, because their brains and bodies feel high from it. It is effortless for them to use their muscles weekly.

I was not one of them. The gym bored me, and like so many others, I quit going after a couple of years. I had made some progress though, developed a few muscles, slight definition, even the beginnings of a six-pack, a four- or five-pack to be honest. But I was done, and I found good excuses, like: no time, too far to drive, family/friend obligations, other things I preferred doing.

Fortunately, I discovered that I loved tennis, especially doubles, and squash for a while. I became passionate about them both, became an enthusiastic player and fan, learning names and games of the top professional tennis players and the best college squash kids. I became a groupie who followed the number one men's college squash team, Trinity, which was an hour away and had an unprecedented streak of 250 consecutive wins, 13 straight national championships. I went to home and away games. It was all quite thrilling.

Now, I can't play too much tennis—love it—doing it two or three times a week, often with "youngsters" in their 50s and 60s, sometimes in their 30s and 40s. I am lucky that I didn't start until my late 60s, so my bones and cartilage aren't all worn down. But I am still struggling to play well enough to keep up or beat the more experienced people in my groups.

I've also morphed into someone who watches matches live and on TV and shares in that whole bonding brotherhood of fans as well. Lucky us. Who'd have ever imagined? But you can't force a sports passion like this. You need the time, the money—although a racket and some clothes are not as much an obstacle as those who want to race cars or compete in horse shows. You need to discover which activity is right for you. It turns out that I am competitive, so pleasurable skiing, swimming, biking, hiking, just don't do it for me. No matter. I've found mine. There are hundreds for you to choose from. Just pick one and go to it.

You may find that if you start exercising your diet will change also. My capoeira master's words were, "I avoid any alcohol, because it is poison to my system." That admonition reduced my wine and beer intake to almost nothing. I also realized that I could perform better if I had a protein shake after a demanding match, became conscious of other foods that might enhance performance, and learned those that were bad for athletics. So more diet and health changes evolved.

A high school classmate who became a doctor told me that based on a 2015 study, 70% of all cancers are random, no known causation. That's not like smoking can give you lung cancer, or eating excessive bad food can lead to obesity, diabetes, illness, cancer or death. Nope. 70% are random. Just bad luck. Is that why so many educated, aware people ignore diet, exercise and health? I mean if all that effort and denial could be for naught, and you are going to get cancer or heart attack anyway—if you are one of the unlucky ones—why deprive yourself, when so many bad foods taste so good? I understand that attitude. But I don't agree with it. I very much want to reduce the odds. Many recent studies have challenged the random/bad luck interpretation and concluded that changes in lifestyle can make a huge difference.

I spent a lot of years in a bathing suit growing up in Miami Beach, Florida. "I see a lot of sun damage here," my Connecticut doctor told me decades later. "You better see a dermatologist every six months." And I did. In 2002, the skin doctor found a deadly skin cancer on my back called melanoma, which was removed before it spread. If I hadn't gone for my biannual check-ups I would likely have died.

It would be great if our bodies stayed healthy and would just wear out at 80 or 90 years old, wouldn't it? But that's not the way things work. Most people want good health, but then you must expend effort to achieve that result.

All goals are realized this way. If you want more money, you work hard and sacrifice for it. To succeed in your career or a major task, you must work hard and sacrifice for it. To enjoy a glowing relationship, you need to give up some things and compromise for it. It's almost the nature of existence. Define your objective. Plan to reach it. Overcome obstacles and setbacks. Keep believing and struggling and attempting to make progress despite those around you who are not supportive and tell you it's not worth the effort. It's not easy. But it's the only way you will succeed.

This strategy certainly applies to maintaining good health, which I mentioned is the most important, highest priority in my life. No one wants to be sick. So how can you not focus on what it takes to increase your stamina and physical well-being? Your body is different from everyone else's. You know—or can learn—what foods give you indigestion or hives or make you queasy. You can cut down on your portion size. You can notice that the first spoonful of your favorite ice cream tastes delicious. But by the fourth mouthful, it isn't as tasty, so you can stop. You can use olive oil, instead of butter. You can drink low fat or almond or soy milk, instead of cow's whole milk. When the vet said my dog was overweight, I simply cut down on how much kibble I give her, and by god she drops a few pounds.

This will work for humans too. Do you really need to drink six beers or three gins? Will you feel any less relaxed if you reduce your alcoholic intake? Make it a game. See if you can overcome these health-harmful habits.

If you don't now exercise regularly, how about taking a weekly walk, build up to a run, or maybe a Zumba or yoga class? At least give it a try. Maybe there is one—just one—physical activity that you can enjoy enough to do it again, and want to do it again, and find that it pleases you so much that you will need to integrate it into your life. I am awed by the man I know who for decades rose at 5:30 AM to hit the gym before he commuted an hour to his office job. It has to be part of his life. I wouldn't wake up that early if I didn't have to. He must feel better from doing it. Maybe you will too.

You must have heard that in life there are no guarantees. When it comes to health, however, there is a guarantee. You will feel better in the short term, you are likely to live longer, move more easily, and be in better shape over time. Your brain will probably think more clearly. You might sleep more restfully. And you will be a more desirable partner.

Those are a lot of benefits from getting your physical act together. Give it a thought. If you are still skeptical, write down the benefits of not taking care of your health. There can't be many. Then ask yourself, "What am I waiting for?" The rest of your life is ahead of you.

CHAPTER NINETEEN

LOVE AND LIVES ARE BLIND AND KIND OF DEAF

Not seeing reality is a common limitation of the human brain, whether it is involving our career, politics, investments and especially when it comes to love.

One afternoon in the early 1980s, I was enjoying a very stimulating party in Washington, DC, when my girlfriend in New York started ovulating and summoned me immediately to return on the next plane, so we could try again to make a baby. We were never successful, thank goodness, but that relationship illustrated how easy it was for me and others to be smitten, Svengalied, mesmerized, and infatuated. Unfortunately, I could not see clearly the reality of who she was: a 42-year-old, never-married career woman who had chosen me as a last resort to give her a child.

I thought I was in love with this woman. She was brilliant, had written a respected book, was fluent in other languages, was a sophisticated global traveler. Even more captivating were her famous and accomplished friends. There I was dining one evening at the home of a former principal dancer of the New York City Ballet, disagreeing on Fire Island with the head of the New York City Teachers Union, enjoying dinner in Sao Paolo with that city's former mayor, discussing politics with a respected author/TV commentator, or culture with a top NY Times editor. I swam with two Rockefellers in their private indoor pool at the family estate in Pocantico Hills, NY.

As stunned and blinded as I was with her entrée and these celebrities, my friends were telling me how I wasn't seeing the problems in our relationship. Finally, my college roommate risked our close friendship and let me know what a stupid jerk I was to continue being with her, and he especially warned me how damaging it would be for the child to be raised without a full-time father. That woke me up.

So I confronted her, and she told me that if she did conceive, maybe we would live together, but it was very unlikely that we would ever marry. I was clear at last about what was happening, and I broke off the relationship with few regrets. But for almost the year we were together, my judgment about her was naïve and clouded.

Three decades later, I was the close friend alerting an infatuated, wealthy buddy that he was missing the clear signals about his relationship. After just two months of dating, my friend had given an expensive engagement ring to a beautiful woman 30 years younger than himself, who was still married, living in an apartment (my friend was never able to visit) on the same floor as her 30-year-older husband whom she didn't want to hurt by initiating a divorce. The young woman asked my friend to also change the deed to his house to include her as a show of good faith.

For months, I challenged him with my suspicions, risking our friendship and adding to his guilt that he wasn't trusting her. A year later, after many of his other friends piled on, he finally accepted that the woman may have been after his money, and he reluctantly broke it off. These days he can't understand how he was so silly and could not have seen what was apparent to his friends.

We all have stories like these that are our own or belong to those we know. Confirmation bias seems to be how our brains work: it's the tendency to interpret new evidence so that it supports and validates one's existing beliefs and ignores or discounts facts that do not support our beliefs. Bias perseverance is when beliefs persist even after the evidence for them is shown to be false. Our brains are either filtering out the facts that will change our opinions or only letting in ideas that back them up.

As you make your daily decisions and especially some biggies that will change the paths and directions of your life, it's critical to know about your brain and how it might be tricking you.

If you are unhappy with your job or boss, you don't want to be in denial. It's stressful. You can always change your attitude to believe that you like your boss or job. But that may not be smart in the long run. You certainly don't want to tune out the reality that you are in a shrinking or dying industry before you lose your ability to make a living. It's hard and upsetting to take steps to make changes, to retrain yourself, identify your most marketable skills, rock the boat and the waters that you and your loved ones are traveling in. But it's essential for your economic survival.

This inherent way our brain functions explains immediately why using logic to convince someone to think differently is such a difficult or impossible task. The facts often don't matter. Psychologists understand this. We are emotional creatures. When we are overloaded with too many stimuli, we resist taking on more input. Words and passions often fall on deaf ears. We strive to retain the balanced outlook that we were taught and learned as youngsters and accepted as we became adults. But the consequences for you in your life can be significant. The stronger your beliefs, the more difficult it is to allow new and conflicting information to change them.

Having or encountering contradictory beliefs creates tension and anxiety. This psychological state, called cognitive dissonance, can occur when we have opposing beliefs or values, perform an action that contradicts our ideas, or confront new information that challenges our beliefs or ideas.

Be aware in love and life that avoiding this tension can lead to some bad decisions.

I learned more precisely what cognitive dissonance is, while watching a documentary about D-Day in the Second World War. The Allies were going to attack German-occupied France from England, the biggest sea invasion in history. The Germans had built defenses all along the northern coast and concentrated the largest portion of their troops and tanks at Calais, the narrowest point in the English Channel between the two countries. From a US deception program and faulty intelligence, the German high command was convinced the attack was coming there. Part of it was that they believed George Patton was the Allies' best general, and he was publicized to oversee the forces in England opposite Calais. The truth was that it was a fake army, had decoy airfields, tanks made of inflatable rubber that looked real from the air.

When the invasion came at Normandy, 200 miles to the west, Hitler and some other top generals were certain that it was a feint, a ruse, so they did not order reinforcements to leave Calais and support Normandy for hours after that battle began. They ignored the facts in front of them and stayed firm in their belief that Calais would be the main attack. They had confirmation bias. They primarily took in the information that supported their initial conclusion, rather than accepting news that challenged it. Drove a lot of their other generals crazy, because they recognized what was happening much sooner. But it was too late. By evening of June 6th, 150,000 Allied troops had landed at Normandy and begun the advance that cost the Germans the war.

Some studies have shown that people are even more determined to persist in their beliefs–despite contradictory evidence–if they've written those beliefs down. I suspect that if one has publicly stated and endorsed those beliefs, it's almost impossible to change what you believe, not just what you say, but what you believe. This is true particularly of politicians and national leaders who make decisions and policies they truly think are correct and are unable to admit they made a mistake—or think they made a mistake—after history has proven them wrong.

You must be on guard. You must pay attention. You need to be willing to adapt, pivot, and change direction. Maybe it helps to write down your conclusions privately and let them sit a few days before making a big decision. Do everything you can to review your situation objectively. Talk with people whom you trust will give you honest feedback. Consider scenarios in which you make the opposite choice you prefer and evaluate how your future looks from that perspective.

You must know the expression, "Don't throw good money after bad." If your car keeps breaking down and needing repairs, then at a certain point you should stop fixing it and buy or lease a new one. It makes more financial sense. Same if you are keeping a failing business afloat with new money that doesn't seem to be saving it from bankruptcy. Or you bought a stock that is now falling, instead of rising, and you keep buying more to average down, instead of cutting your losses and moving on to a more promising venture.

These might be examples of not taking in the facts and being fooled by confirmation bias. You latch onto wishful thinking to support your initial views about how it's beneficial to spend more money. Yet at some point, hopefully, you wake up to the truth.

There are so many movies and novels, where the main

character doesn't see his idiocy. You almost want to scream out loud in the theater, "Don't do it!" "Stop!" "Are you crazy?" If we can recognize the stupidity in others, maybe we can learn to catch ourselves from such delusions, denials and poor choices.

Remember, your brain is set up to trick you. It doesn't want internal conflict and tension. Stress is destabilizing. Thus, you are inclined to take the easier path, even if it is not the best path. You have to fight that basic mental laziness. Success here will be the best choice for you.

CHAPTER TWENTY

CONSIDER ASIAN PHILOSOPHIES AND MARTIAL ARTS STRATEGIES

When I was in high school, my chiropractor father bought a Chinese acupuncture doll that showed all the junctions of meridians on the body, and where the needles were supposed to be inserted. This was maybe 20 years before acupuncture was legal in the States. My father only used his thumbs to apply pressure at the right places.

I had grown up hearing him called a quack, because his profession was not recognized by medical doctors. I had also heard countless dinner table tales about patients whose ailments, aches, and infirmities continued after years of visits with normal MDs and other health professionals, until in desperation they decided to give my dad a chance. Within days or weeks they felt better or could walk or move a limb without pain.

The quack wasn't so crazy.

During those same years, my mother started doing yoga, again decades before you could join a class in your local gym or church group. This was a rare Indian discipline that I learned about from hard-to-find books she shared showing a thin guy in a loincloth contorted like a pretzel.

During my high school years, I learned about Japanese culture, and I decided I wanted to marry a geisha—I didn't know that geishas didn't marry. I even started meditating in a full lotus position. By the time I was a sophomore in college, I was showing off these skills and interests. I meditated on the floor of the landing of my fraternity house, indifferent to the chaos around me. I slept on a wooden door covered only with a sheet. I won lots of praise when an unknowing frat brother sat on my 'bed' and almost broke his tailbone.

Growing up in a Judeo-Christian culture, we are taught our versions of right and wrong, the lessons of the two bibles (old and new), the 10 Commandments. But the rest of the world has also been living and learning how to conduct a few billions of lives and gleaning some knowledge of what works and doesn't. So why not benefit from all that history and human experience, I reasoned. It made incredibly good sense. Maybe there are some guidelines in Asian philosophies I could use along my path and journey.

I wanted to achieve, impress, be a success, find happiness, earn money, make a difference. Being of an open mind and having a loving heart, the more wisdom the better. If I learned a few things that others didn't know—having extra arrows in my quiver, as some say in rural America—I would have a real advantage over those limited by the smaller range of merely Western choices.

Each year over 130 million people are born. We have different genes, health, privileges, parents, bodies, upbringings, opportunities. We need to figure out our strengths and capitalize on them. We also need to figure out our weak points as well, so we can improve them or delegate those challenges to others. Then we are all in the same clash to become successful. Sometimes it is a contest against thousands, like a high school grad applying to a large university. Other times it is against hundreds, like an actor going for a part and an artist wanting her work to be purchased by a museum. On a rare occasion it is against a few, like a top executive competing for her company's presidency.

Repeatedly, we are in this mix of striving to win a prize. In almost every case there are people involved somewhere.

Even the solitary artist or writer still must deal with the gallery owner, publisher, agent, curator, public. Because of this, it is helpful, if not essential, to learn as much as you can about how human nature works, and not just Western nature.

Meditation has taught me that I could control my body in a surprising way. Before tests in college, I would breathe to calm myself and minimize my nervous anxiety.

When I was in the army, I took a stress test that had me running on a treadmill. To tease the doctor measuring my heart rate and pulse after a few minutes, I closed my eyes, breathed deeply and shocked him: my heart rate had barely changed.

After military service, where I had saved enough money to read for eight months in Manhattan, I studied a lot of Zen Buddhism. I discovered Eugen Herrigel's, *Zen in the Art of Archery*. I cherished Alan Watts', *The Book*, which was written simply for his children and grandchildren and is based on Vedanta Hinduism. There were many other books. George Leonard's *The Ultimate Athlete* was a game changer, and had a fabulous bibliography.

Herrigel tells us to release the bowstring as gently as a baby lets go of your finger or as the snow falls suddenly off the bamboo leaf. He writes of how breathing transforms into "being breathed." He asks his master how to become purposeless on purpose? Mostly, he learns to eliminate his ego and his achievement, so that the man and the art and the work all become one. But what good is this advice in my everyday world, I wondered, if I am not hunting or target shooting with a bow and arrow? And what is meant by surrendering to win? How does that work? Or reading that there can't be black without white?

Well, I created a good life around some of these principles and made a lot of money as well. You can too, for sure.

I saw a horse whisperer once take a completely wild mustang and ride him on a saddle within an hour. It may have been a fraud at the rodeo, but I have since read that it is possible. What I learned is that if you are gentle instead of brutal and forceful, you can train the animal quickly. Attract the flies with honey.

If you walk toward a horse, he will walk backwards, away from you. But when I face the horse and walk backwards, a form of surrender, then the horse comes towards me—a win. People don't understand that surrendering isn't a bad thing. People would rather have you work with them than against them.

You have probably heard about the couple who gave up after years of trying to have a baby, decided to adopt, and then became pregnant. My mother had five miscarriages after me, before she gave up, thought she'd reached menopause and then conceived my brother, who is 16 years younger.

After 8-9 years of being single following my divorce, I looked unsuccessfully for a partner for 3-4 years, finally gave up, accepted single-hood and dating, resigned to flings and living alone, and then found my wife.

I have given up hoping to sell a house in a recession after years of trying, and then received the broker call reporting an out-of-the-blue offer that later closed.

How does this happen again and again? I understand if I am too pushy, turn someone off or away and lose a job or a sale. But I can't grasp the desired result, when I am not involved directly in the outcome. Is the 'Universal Omnipotence' granting me my wish, when I am humble? I have no idea. I just know that it works. Try it, but of course you really have to give up. No pretending you're defeated. No cheating allowed.

After my divorce, I searched for spiritual answers. I had friends in Los Angeles who took me to a huge auditorium to listen to a professional channeler, I had my past lives revealed in a sort of hypnotic session and learned that I had been a pirate and an Egyptian belly dancer.

None of these explorations transformed me or influenced me greatly. They were tasty tidbits on the smorgasbord table of my life. Glad I did them, lots of fun, and I'd recommend them for anyone.

Then I was persuaded to go to a weekend workshop in New York State with Swami Muktananda, the guru's guru, who had attracted media stories and stars, like Jerry Brown, the former California governor, John Denver, James Taylor, Carly Simon, astronaut Edgar Mitchell. I remember during one group meditation that with eyes closed, I "saw" white light streaming out of my stomach like a fire hose. Arousing this kundalini energy was one of this guru's great gifts. I read that he was also known for teaching followers to "see god in each other" and "the god within you is you."

This reminded me of the Jewish belief that there is a bit of god inside each person, and it is one's obligation to enhance that godliness and to make it more apparent.

That weekend with Muktananda was powerful. Its positive effects were only slightly marred when years later it turned out that this famous, respected spiritual leader was constantly violating his pronouncements of celibacy and having frequent sex with many of his female followers.

However, all those experiences did teach me what is obvious to many: there is a definite mind-body connection. You affect your body, then your mind is changed too, and vice versa. Obviously if you drink or smoke grass, your brain is muddled and affected. It is not as obvious if your brain is troubled, say by stress and anxiety, then it affects your health and physical well-being.

I had grown up with this perspective, because my father preached that much illness was psychosomatic. He saw these direct connections all the time.

Richard Strozzi-Heckler. Aikido master.

Richard Strozzi-Heckler, a close California friend even taught this view to students, gave workshops, and wrote books about it. He was greatly informed about Asian philosophy. I met him because he was an advanced black-belt master in the Japanese martial art of aikido, which I had taken up (and studied for three years) in New York City. On a California business trip, I went to his dojo, and my life was changed forever.

I've already described how aikido, unlike other martial arts, does not meet force with force. You don't block a punch with your arm to stop the attacker's arm. Instead you blend with the enemy and get out of the way.

Aikido is often translated to mean the way of unifying (with) life energy or as "the way of harmonious spirit." You may defend yourself while not injuring your attacking enemy. You simply want to control his actions. When he tries to hit you, you dodge and pivot 180 degrees, so you are side-by-side, he misses you and hits nothing, but is greatly off balance. Now you push down on his falling arm, and his own momentum helps bring him to the floor. Then you disable him.

Although aikido is very physical, it is also very spiritual. It is not meant to be utilized in a cave away from civilization. It is meant to help us interact with the world and its people...especially its people, and I don't mean in a martial way. I built a business that led to affluence using these principles. I created relationships with relatives, friends and even strangers following this outlook. And it has been astonishingly successful.

I loved discovering this way of dealing with the real world. And this is what I am suggesting that you search for yourself: life path attitudes that are outside of what you learned from your parents and growing up in the West. There is much that we can learn from the East.

When a disciple of aikido's founder came from Japan to NY for a workshop, he predictably shared some techniques for disarming opponents on the dojo mat. However, his biggest impact on me was saying that he thanked each grain of rice for giving up its life to nourish him. Thanking god or your horse or your dog I could relate to immediately. But a grain of rice was a mindblower back then.

I have since learned there is a Buddhist practice called the "thankfulness or gratitude meditation." You don't have to sit in a lotus position with your legs crossed properly to appreciate the good things in your life. You can do it riding on the bus or walking in the street. No matter how many problems you have, there must be some blessings that you can focus on to change your sour mood or feelings of hopelessness. I find myself being thankful many times a week.

It used to be when I was in a funk that I would just wait it out. Taking on the old theory that, "This too shall pass." But martial arts and Asian practices have helped me refocus my energy. To turn my negative thoughts into something positive.

Richard, my aikido friend, also introduced me to a Brazilian martial art called capoeira, considered one of the deadliest in the world, totally the opposite of aikido. One of the great masters of that art, Bira Almieda, called a gladiator in Rio, had moved to San Francisco in 1978 and been challenged by many of the most skilled practitioners of various martial arts there. I heard he beat them all. I attended a session and was so entranced that I gave up aikido and studied capoeira for the next three years in New York.

There are a lot of kicks, squats, jumps, handstands and cartwheels in this sport. These moves are done to music and singing by onlookers waiting their turn. I believe it was invented by Brazilian slaves from Africa who were prohibited from fighting at all. So they disguised their practice sessions by dancing inside a circle of their buddies who were clapping and playing special musical instruments (drums, tambourines, a cowbell, a plucked, one-string bow). In combat, they held razor blades in their toes and gave powerful kicks that could break bones and knock heads unconscious.

At age 42, I was 20 years older than most of the others. I was also one of the few white guys in the group. My friends there were often students, unemployed or one was an unlicensed street peddler running daily from the police. One time a classmate who'd been in a neighborhood fight worried that he had killed or permanently disabled someone with a kick he'd practiced. I arrived at sessions from my office on 5th Avenue and 57th Street, sometimes after a photography gallery opening with suits and art collectors. It was a bizarre contrast. But I learned about disguise, joy, being fluid, the carefree Brazilian attitude and music. I became more familiar with Carnival and samba and passions and superstitions. Those capoeira years were some of my best moments ever, especially when we traveled to Brazil together with our mestre (teacher).

I learned a lot about other cultures when I visited exotic places like India, Korea, Soviet Union, Bhutan and La Dakh. In Moscow, a bureaucrat taught me that "success has many fathers, but failure is an orphan." If you let other people take some credit for your good idea (rather than keeping it all to yourself), then you have a greatly improved chance of its becoming a success. Most people want the glory all for themselves. Many are also afraid to delegate to others who are more capable. I am exactly the opposite, partly because my ego doesn't need as much stroking: the more credit I give to others, the more they feel appreciated and enjoy working with/for me. And the more often I work with people more experienced or capable than myself, the easier it is for me to move on to the next issue, see the bigger picture, manage my company and my life more proficiently.

That's just me. I learned to know (many parts of) myself. This was advice from ancient Greece, and I took it. Make a list of YOUR strengths and weaknesses. You may surprise yourself; then deal with it.

CHAPTER TWENTY-ONE

PRACTICAL WISDOM

Wisdom is the ability to think and act using knowledge, experience, understanding, common sense and insight. If you can organize all this information and feeling, you will have a huge edge in reaching all your goals. Especially if they are very concrete efforts to make money, pivot or reinvent yourself.

I only met Yoko Ono once for about two minutes in the 1970s. She was still married to John Lennon and had just come out of an "est" seminar in Manhattan. I asked her if it was worth signing up, and she said, "Why not? It was only two weekends in your life."

I went to an introductory session after my first wife had taken this popular self-help program back then and changed considerably. Our marriage was in trouble, so she tried it. I took Yoko's advice and followed them both.

I came away with one very important suggestion: **avoid expectations.** If you have them, and they don't materialize, you will be very disappointed. Give them up. A bit like the Buddhists saying if you eliminate desire, many of your problems will evaporate. In fact, the founder of est, Werner Erhard, explained that Zen Buddhism was the biggest influence in developing est, which stands for Erhard Seminars Training.

Making your desires go away seems a lot more difficult to me than just not expecting how the future will turn out. You can never know in advance what's going to happen. Doesn't mean you can't wish or hope for good things or get excited about some possibility. Many people I know control their enthusiasm in case they are let down. Not me. The night before a critical interview, key meeting or when a contract might be signed, I love to relish the tension and promise. I just don't know the outcome. I don't count on it succeeding. I never forget that it might not happen, so I never expect a certain conclusion. I simply long for it and think how happy I will be if the deal or test or whatever I want comes true.

Naturally, I am not thrilled when the results don't go my way, but at least I had those few hours of excitement the night before.

Not having expectations, certainly applies to anticipating how people will behave. I find you can't count on most strangers or predict their responses. I have learned from experience, that I have some friends and relatives who will come through in supportive ways or at least give me an honest, non-diplomatic, non-politically correct opinion, when I ask for it. These folks are blessings in my life. Do you have these sorts of people in your life? Hopefully, you do.

When you have years, maybe decades, of noticing that people let you down, it makes sense not to have expectations of how they are going to act. Why set yourself up for another disappointment?

I want to assure you I know that just passing on tidbits of wisdom does not make it easy to follow my suggestions. Especially, in the heat of an emotional moment. When your hormones are flowing, and raw nerves are being poked; when you're being squeezed by someone who negotiates in bad faith; when someone is not playing by the rules of the game as you understand them.

However that's the jungle we live in.

You can seek to be surrounded by honest, decent people. You can only hire or work with folks you admire and respect. But an indifferent bureaucrat or insurance adjuster or overtaxed policeman just might not bend to your preferences, and certainly a natural disaster, like a flood or hurricane, isn't paying attention to your likes and dislikes. Life is tough, and people are messy.

When I was just a toddler, my mother taught me that, **"Life isn't fair."** Years later, when I told an artist's representative that his trade association was trying to make things fairer for all reps by instituting new rules for a level playing field, he said he didn't want that change. He liked having an upper hand that fed more jobs to him instead of his competitors. This is reality.

Knowing fairness doesn't prevail and not expecting things to be fair is a real advantage in achieving calm and equanimity amidst chaos. It's also a benefit in dealing with the crappy, unfair situation, because you are not as surprised or upset, not as flabbergasted or enraged, and you have a start at making better decisions to deal with the bramble you just discovered you are in.

I find it helps to be neutral and to not raise my voice. I may want to punish someone, but I would never use violence. Even though, I once thought of hiring a private detective, because I had the desire to beat someone up once I found the guy.

That happened when I sold a man's company and looked to the seller for my finder's fee commission. I'd searched for the buyer for years. After the deal money changed hands, and the seller was a multi-millionaire, he told me to get lost. He sold his house, sold his restaurant, divorced his wife, bought a big boat and began cruising the Gulf of Mexico. I was not happy to say the least; not fair!

But my case was so good that a lawyer took it on contingency. We reached that scoundrel seller (I'd helped make rich) via ship-to-shore radio, and five years later, he settled. Vengeance is mine, even if I ended up with considerably less than our contract had stated.

I know how unfair life can be. Although, my example was not devastating. I'll bet you have a few that can top it. We all do. Everyone has their story. I've gone years without sleeping easily, up at 5:30 AM, terrified that I was going to be bankrupt as the result of an unwarranted lawsuit by a European business partner who was simply toying with me and attempting to take away my stock and rights without paying adequately for them.

Worse than that are the people born with deformities or illnesses or become seriously or deathly sick at young/ middle ages. There are children who lose their parents, refugees. Kids who can't afford college. People pummeled by alcoholic fathers. Innocents fleeced by con artists. Those who just can't get 'a break.' The woman in the Lower East Side who was robbed at gun point and told the crook sarcastically that he wasn't going to use his gun; and then he shot and killed her.

Life is not fair. But as I said earlier, it's all how you deal with your problems and your burdens. You can say that there is always someone worse off than you, and feel better knowing that. You can look up at other people better off and try to join them. You can accept your limitations and bad early experiences and use that reality to make the most with what you have and who you are. You can stop crying that life is unfair, and you got a bum rap.

Even so, when a respected rabbi I knew retired after decades of leadership in his congregation, I was pained to hear that six months later he discovered that he had cancer. Two weeks after that, he died. I still can't easily accept the unfairness of that story. I try to follow my own advice, but here is a religious, spiritual revered man who is cut down soon after just beginning the next phase of a giving and holy life.

It's a small injustice compared to the hundreds of millions who die prematurely, by wars, disease, natural disasters, and so on. There are so many unfair events all around us all the time. So much randomness. So little control. So much uncertainty.

The Buddhists (again) have another way of framing the problem: **pretend that you are the sky,** and that you are calmly, watching the clouds go by: nice fluffy puffs of white, even though they are your problems, storms, antagonists, setbacks, personal failures and disasters.

I love this picture.

I also like the image of **humans as air molecules near the tire nozzle.** It's been with me for much of my life. I learned in high school how tire pressure is made up of zillions of air molecules moving around constantly and colliding with each other, and the inside of the tire. Keeps the tire inflated. But every now and then, an 'outer force' comes along, unscrews the nozzle cap, and lets some air out of the tire.

Think of yourself as being one of those happy air molecules inside the tire, but who just happened to be near the nozzle at the exact instant the nozzle was depressed to let out some air, and you are now released from inside the tire into the outer air. It's totally random. No one ever told you that there was a nozzle to the outside. No one ever told you that sometimes the nozzle is depressed. No one ever told you that you should steer clear of the nozzle in case it is depressed and going to change your life forever. It's random. You can call it luck: bad if you were happy inside the tire, good if you were bored there and wanted a change.

But your life as an air molecule is now changed forever, and drastically. You are not to blame. You can't do anything about it. You are smart to adapt to your new circumstances. Because you can't go back to the old life, ever.

That's why it's best to **appreciate and enjoy the good moments while you have them. Never forget that your life is always going to change.** You will marry and maybe divorce. Take on the joys of children, along with their frustrations. Loved ones will die. You will lose jobs. Be forced to relocate. Suffer financial losses. Have health issues. Have to compromise with others. It's all inherent in being human and being alive. Once you grasp this reality, your life will be different.

Everywhere you go, you see people getting upset, because their coffee is cold, a stranger didn't smile at them, they weren't invited to a party. You need to keep these disappointments in perspective. I was bemoaning an aching elbow from playing too much tennis one month. Then I reconnected with a close high school friend and learned that he has lung cancer and just finished six months of chemotherapy. How puny my aches are. If I have to cut back or stop playing tennis, it's a lot better than being dead! I better change my attitude immediately and enjoy all of life's pleasures and satisfactions while I can. Right?

However, just knowing what to do is a long way from doing it. I know I need to watch the tennis ball, but it's still very hard to do. If we must practice, and practice perfectly, to improve a tennis swing, we must practice diligently to better appreciate and improve our lives.

Hearing or saying some words is only the first step in taking new actions. I knew a young waitress who told me she used to be an entertainment "critica" in college back in Cuba. I asked her if she had tried to get into that business here in the states. She said that she hadn't. I asked her why not and she said: "I am too shy." I introduced her to a friend of mine in the theater world, but I reminded her that no one is coming to restaurants looking for movie and drama critics. She has to put herself out there. She needs to take a risk.

Taking a risk is an essential part of a human's growth. When taking a risk there is always a chance of failing. However if you succeed, there is not just the opportunity for reward, but you will also overcome your fears. You need to make whatever degree of effort you are capable of at this point in your evolution towards becoming as fulfilled and successful as you can. Write the letter, ask the girl out, apply for the job, call on the new customer. No matter what your tolerance for risk is, strive for it, put in some time. That is the only way to progress.

While you are evolving, **notice the phases of your life:** Relish their beginnings, accept their completion, and move on to the next stage. When I was 21, carrying my parachute back to the staging area after my fifth and final military jump as part of a four-week training program, I knew that walking down that red-clay, dusty road in the hot Georgia sun was the last moments of a great exploit and lifetime memory. I was savoring every second and can still see myself there. I had watched people break shoulders from a two-foot-high practice jump. I had heard about jumpers who broke their legs upon landing in soft ground and the men who died from an updraft that pushed them into propellers of planes above and behind them.

But I knew what I had to do, and I jumped, survived and moved on. I loved jumping. Exhilarating, thrilling moments in my life; and although each jump was a risk, I reveled in it as that adventure flew by. However, I don't live in the past, wishing that I could be back then forever. But I have friends who talk about their glory days in high school as the years that were the best in their lives. They are stuck in another time. I wonder if they were prescient enough to focus on those early years as fantastic and irreplaceable when they were living them?

I remember when my first marriage was ending, and I moved out of the bedroom. The old days were over, the happy times with that wife were behind me. I grieved for months, but I recognized that another phase had ended, and I had to mourn for it and move on. Just like when I was fired from jobs, or leaving Korea after a year of military duty there. We all have to push ahead, live in the present, and accept the future. It's just being mindful and aware. And it happens over and over. For all of us, if to different degrees.

I have had five or six careers. I met an 87-year-old cardiologist who had the same career his entire life. He was married to the same woman for decades, until she died. It was so hard for him, but eight years after her passing, he began seeing someone new. Because even though we may not like it, we all have these changes. I simply advise you to be prepared for them, enjoy your various phases if you can, never assume that they will go on forever, and accept that most will end no matter how hard you fight their inevitable termination.

Shove the "should do's" is one of the best recommendations I ever received. Dump them right over a cliff. The message is to connect with what truly matters to you, so that you can incorporate those preferences in your life. Whatever effort it takes. There will be parents, bosses, peers, colleagues, centuries of tradition, and maybe even laws that all attempt to tell you what you should do and shape you differently than you want to behave or act. Mythologist and writer Joseph Campbell said to "Follow your bliss." But it is more than just bliss or passion, it is following a lifestyle of what works specifically for you.

There are scores of choices we make in our lives that result in our being happier or dissatisfied with ourselves. The beliefs of the culture we come from and live in all dictate how we "should" behave. The great challenge is to identify what we prefer, rather than simply selecting what others expect us to do and insist that we must or should do. I am not thinking only of big decisions, like having kids, picking where to live, your job or education. Those are horribly confronting if your parents are urging you to give them grandchildren, before you feel ready. Or friends are telling you how perfect your high school sweetheart is for a wife. Or loved ones are insisting you shouldn't leave them and move to greater job opportunities in the big city.

There are also the smaller daily selections that add up to who we are and what kind of life we are living. Our clothes, food, friends, music, morals, sports, hobbies. It is easier for a teen, rather than the average working adult, to wear torn jeans, blackened fingernails, and display pierced body parts. Maybe there are less extreme clothing styles that you like. But I know a woman who told her boyfriend how to dress and slapped him in the face, because he didn't bring to Europe a perfectly normal sport jacket she wanted him to wear there. Ridiculous. I remember a man in the army who criticized people who ate salad. Humans were meant to eat meat, he insisted, not grass, like cows and horses. Absurd. So was the criticism I used to receive growing up for eating raw fish, before sushi was popular in America, and playing ping pong and bowling, instead of football or other team sports.

If you are constantly facing these kinds of annoying pressures of how you are supposed to behave and what you should like, you know they drain your confidence and spirit. They can suck away your vitality as you are stuffed into someone else's mold. But if you want to defy these expectations and do resist or fight back, you will ultimately be much happier, maybe even jubilant.

The first requirement is to figure out or feel what you want, truly prefer. About anything. Then practice doing "your thing" in small, less significant mediums, like food choices, an article of clothing or two, maybe a school course or concert event. Watch a movie you think appeals to your blossoming self. Or read a book you may have been afraid to have been seen carrying.

Little steps, tiny, less confrontational moves to give you sure-footedness for the times you might someday take on longer "hikes" or climbing mountains of peer-group opposition. It's surely easier for an artist like author Philip Roth to ignore the Jewish leaders who urged him not to write about seamy, less attractive sides of Jewish life. But with practice, you can find your own path too. You can move on to a different, more accepting bevy of buddies, who welcome and appreciate who you have become. Best of all, you will be overjoyed, satisfied and like who you have become. Fantastic.

Stay focused on your vision. Don't be diverted or sidetracked by less important encounters with people who obstruct, ridicule or discourage you. Also, don't let your own ego block your progress. You may have to swallow your pride, lose face, or compromise during the journey. You may want to make a deal to reach your goal or destination.

I am a firm believer in making concessions. You may disagree, thinking that it's essential to be tough or act like a macho guy. It's true that some Middle Eastern cultures— and even some extreme American political groups—

believe that compromise is unforgivable. A total violation of one's principles. But when others are involved with differing views, styles, and values, you must find common ground and mutual benefits, if you want the assistance of those other people to help you reach your endpoint.

If you stay focused on your main goal, maintain a vision of where you want to go or what you want to achieve, then the obstructions, the bumps in the road or abuse you encounter can be dealt with much better. It's super important to remember that people are not rational much of the time. They tend to be emotional. In the heat of an argument, or new and uncomfortable idea or proposal, they are grappling with psychological difficulty and frequently strike back with words of anger or frustration. I ignore the meaning of those words and stay calm, do not react predictably by raising my voice, or take the bait and escalate our conversation into a dispute.

Human egos are incredibly fragile and easily alarmed and disrupted. If you are negotiating, you want others to be as reasonable as possible as you try to win them closer to your side. You never want to tell them that they are wrong or aren't perceptive, or have to change their ways to your ways. You can't embarrass or humiliate them, so they lose face or prestige with their peers. You need to be patient, see things from their point of view, and identify what benefits they can gain by doing what you want. And then at some point, a deal can be made. I was once in negotiations that took 20 hours of mediating before we made any progress. Sometimes it takes months to find the middle ground for agreement. Always it takes focus on what the end goal is.

The best news is that you can practice interacting with people every day—in stores, on the phone, at work. Teach yourself how to stay calm, maybe by taking subtle deep breaths, keeping a mental picture of yourself a step closer to your objective. Believe you can succeed. Because you can. Keep at it. Never give up.

Lastly, always remember, **you can make a difference**. You may feel that you are all alone. Nevertheless, there are countless stories about one person who spoke up or fought for change and was ultimately successful. Whether in reaching an individual goal or helping establish a new law or changing social behavior. These real life examples have been very inspirational for me.

When I google the names of people who made a difference, stars like Jesus and Buddha head the top 100 lists. Few of us will achieve such lofty, planetary influence, but we can still strive to do our best and be very influential and effective.

One of my great inspirations was Peggy Charren. In the 1960s, Saturday morning TV was basically cartoons and rampant commercials that all sold toys and sugared foods, instead of educational and more beneficial programs.

Peggy was very upset that this is what her daughter was exposed to, so she gathered some friends in her living room in 1968 to figure out what they might do. She formed an organization that grew to 10,000 strong, and after years of meetings with broadcasters, congress persons, and other government leaders saw the enactment of the Children's Television Act of 1990. It limited commercials to 12 minutes an hour and spelled out some standards of required educational quality.

An interesting side benefit was that the CBS Senior VP in charge of programming heard her desires in 1970 and resigned soon after to take a 75% pay cut as VP of the Children's Television Workshop, which was producing a new show called *Sesame Street*.

There are many people like Peggy, and you can be one of them. No matter how old you are. There are scores of late bloomers, like Grandma Moses who started painting in her late 70s, Colonel Sanders who started KFC at age 65, and Frank McCourt author of *Angela's Ashes*, who wrote his first novel at 63 and won the Pulitzer Prize three years later.

I think about social activist Jody Williams who started raising awareness about landmines around the world. In 1992, she created the International Campaign to Ban Landmines and took it from a staff of one, herself, to an organization of 1,300 NGOs in ninety countries. In 1997, she and the ICBL were awarded the Nobel Peace Prize just three weeks after a treaty was signed by 122 countries; 164 countries have now signed on.

Alex's Lemonade Stand Foundation is a great story of a young person making a difference. Alexandra Scott had cancer before she was one. At four, after a stem cell transplant, she told her parents that she was going to raise money for doctors, so they could help other kids with cancer. Within a year, she and her brother had raised $2000 selling lemonade. People heard about her mission and created their own lemonade stands. By the time she died four years later in 2004, over $1 million had been raised to help find a cure for her kind of cancer. Since then, over $150 million has been raised to fund research and support families who have kids with cancer. Amazing, isn't it?

I had lunch in my late 20s with Max Ways, a senior editor of *Fortune Magazine*, which back then was one of the leading business publications. Max was in his 60s. I was working at financial public relations, seeing how dishonest and greedy and selfish top corporate executives were for some of the nation's largest corporations.

"How can you write articles about ethics?" I asked him. I've written speeches for these guys, witnessed their lack of morals, decency and concern. You are talking to hypocrites who can't possibly care what you think.

I never forgot his answer and have integrated it into my life since then: "You have two choices. You can shrug your shoulders, turn your back and walk away. Or you can throw your pebble in the pond and make some ripples."

My ten-year-old daughter had nightmares about nuclear war in the early 1980s, when the USSR was an "Evil Empire" in those Cold War days. I decided to visit the country to see what I could do to promote peace. I became one of many "Citizen Diplomats."

I found a group at Esalen, a New Age California community, that was going to Moscow to study psi phenomena (telepathy, remote viewing, using only your mind to move physical objects). I was invited to piggy-back on their trip. Some Soviets who taught the Russian language to US Army troops in San Francisco role-played with us to train us in negotiating with Soviets.

I went to Moscow, Siberia, Georgia, Kazakhstan and saw that ordinary Soviets were warm and wonderful people. It was the government that had to change. I approached some friends I knew who had produced a photography book about Australia that had pictures by 50 photographers all taken in one day, and told them they should do one about the USSR.

They told me it was impossible. They had tried to arrange it through *National Geographic*, *Time*, *Associated Press*, the US Embassy and struck out. I was not deterred. For three years, I wrote letters and contacted people I had met on my first trip in 1984. I wasn't getting anywhere. Fortunately, Mikhail Gorbachev came into power in 1985 and welcomed a more open policy. We finally received permission to move forward.

In 1987, after I and my friends had made a trip to Moscow to work out the terms of our collaboration, we returned to photograph, *A Day In the Life of the Soviet Union*. Prior to this project, no more than four Western photographers had ever been allowed in the country at one time; now there were 50 from the West and another 50 Eastern Bloc photographers. The pictures were developed and edited in Spain. No censorship by any of the picture editors.

The book was one of the top-selling picture books of the year, over 500,000 copies. *Time Magazine* ran a 38-page cover story of these extraordinary photos. There were countless other print stories and radio/ TV interviews as well, so that perhaps 250 million people saw the images. The heads of the US and USSR received copies of the book. People all over the world softened their impressions of what everyday Soviets were like. We broke down barriers for the first time in history. Even those of Soviet citizens, who had never seen these pictures of their comrades living across 11 time zones.

My daughter's nightmares about a nuclear war spurred a project that clearly changed the world's thinking. I ignored the anonymous postcard that called me a communist after I was interviewed on radio and television. I had ignored the concerns of my father, who feared that the US Government would shut down my publishing company for meddling. In fact, State Department officials were quietly encouraging us citizen diplomats to do work that they couldn't do.

I proved to myself that one person could truly make a difference. People can change the world, if they believe passionately in their cause and are willing to put considerable effort into making it happen. It will be a challenge. There will be obstacles. But if you follow some of my advice, it may all just work out for you. C'mon. Now it's your turn. It's your time. Life is fragile and short. You only live it once. Give it a shot.

ABOUT the AUTHOR

Author Ira Shapiro

Ira Shapiro has had several careers in his 78 years of life, and because of that he has learned more than a thing or two.

Ira attended Carnegie Mellon in Pittsburgh, majoring in chemistry. In his junior year, he realized he only liked the subject because of the colors and smells of the lab, but he stayed with it anyway and never ended up taking a job in the field. After college, he hitchhiked five months around America and British Columbia, supporting himself with odd jobs, like selling pizza at the Seattle World's Fair.

He then joined the army: became a paratrooper, served a year in Korea, visited Japan for the first of 20 times, learned he liked to write, and came home on a stretcher with hepatitis he'd contracted volunteering in Korea's largest orphanage.

With his army savings, he moved to New York City, spent seven months in museums and libraries, and studied Greek drama, psychology, the Bible, stock investments, ancient Egypt, how to learn, Zen Buddhism, and Asian-Indian philosophy.

In 1965, he married and had two daughters. He worked briefly as a science textbook editor, handled public relations for a publishing company, and eight years for a PR agency, mainly writing speeches, producing annual reports and hiring some of the country's top journalistic photographers. Then he was fired.

He spent two years running the Nikon photo gallery in New York, handling all PR for Nikon, and meeting many of the country's top commercial photographers, until Nikon fired him. He still couldn't seem to get things 'right.' Until he helped start up and publish a fine art photography tabloid newspaper that survived five issues over two years.

In 1975, he started his own PR firm with photo and color lab accounts. Simultaneously, he launched a visual book publishing company that for over 27 years primarily produced annual directories marketing commercial photographers, illustrators, and graphic designers and a picture magazine for ad agency art directors.

The directories became the biggest color annuals printed by the world's largest printer. In 1996, he published an avant-garde art book that excludes painting and sculpture, and was adopted for years by college professors.

After his separation and divorce from his wife (1980), he frequently traveled around the world for business and vacations. Japan, Bali, Iceland, Europe, India, Ladakh, Hong Kong and South America were among his hot spots in those days.

From 1984 to 1987, Ira was concerned about nuclear war with Reagan's "Evil Empire." He visited the Soviet Union and was the catalyst to produce *A Day in the Life of the Soviet*

Union, which was a photographic portrait of the USSR during 24 hours by 100 photographers, half from Western countries. This was the first time more than four non-Iron Curtain photojournalists had been allowed in the Soviet Union at the same time. The book was one of the biggest selling (540,000 copies) picture books of 1987. Photos from the shoot were seen via TV and print media by an estimated 250 million people, including a 38-page *Time Magazine* cover story.

In 1987, Ira met an artist's representative through business, Jacqueline Dedell. They were married in 1988 and have a son and a daughter. Together Jacqueline and Ira have:

1. Moved to rural Connecticut full time in 1990 to breed about 150 ponies, sheep and goats. Moved again in 2002 to a smaller farm that makes apple cider and maple syrup, breeds endangered Cleveland Bay horses and has peacocks, goats, parrots, 30 politically correct chickens, 50 white pigeons, exotic pheasants, and used to have a black Yucatan pig named Paco.

2. Started a tableware design company named Smashing Plates that (for five years) manufactured plates and stemware in Europe that were distributed throughout America.

3. Co-founded a start-up, Take Two Interactive Software, in 1993 with a 21-year-old that first published travel CD-ROMs and in 2018 was valued at over $15 billion producing the Grand Theft Auto and other video games.

4. Launched a renovation and land preservation business in 1995 that specializes in restoring 18th and 19th century homes and prevents farms from being turned into

developments.

5. Co-founded in 2005, another start-up, Phizzle, which created software that enabled sports teams and venues like Madison Square Garden to reach their fans' cell phones; then morphed into a big data company that has now invented an edge computing solution and an in-memory database architecture and middleware that can ingest and analyze large volumes of real-time transactions a second with minimal hardware and advance the internet of things (IoT).

6. Met astronauts, planetary scientists and rocket engineers at the 2016 World View Inc. opening in Tucson of the world's first dedicated space port for stratospheric balloon launches. World View, Ursa Major, Iceye and Nanoracks are start-ups in the NewSpace—or private spaceflight—industry that Ira and Jacqueline are excited about and investing in.

After many years on the boards of a land trust and a colonial building preservation trust, Ira is now semi-retired and has more time to see his children and three grandchildren, write a book, and to play: he went white water rafting in New

Ira Shapiro. Easter Island.

Zealand; enjoyed wildlife and Buddhist culture in Bhutan; became a passionate tennis player; joined scientists in Mongolia to observe and help band wild cranes; visited Easter Island; and enjoyed star gazing and trekking in the Atacama Desert in Chile.

Thanks To:

Jacqueline Dedell, my wife, for her vision, daring and dynamic partnership for 32 years. "We are an effective team!"

Joe Adler for his enthusiasm and interest in my projects, especially the creation of this book. During 70 years of close friendship, his stirring, unconventional viewpoints and his intense passion for life energized and influenced me magnificently.

Lindsay Preston for her brilliant editing, new chapter ideas and candid contributions to my social media efforts.

Harry Moses for suggesting the title and subtitle.

Andy Merson for his valued advice...again...and his generous support and encouragement of a softback edition.

Friends whose writing achievements motivated me to believe, "If they can do it, then I can too."

Dave Colmar for using his digital expertise and good sense to wend me through the constant complexities of producing a newsletter, website and various versions of my book.

The team at Strikepoint Media—Brent Blossom, Rodrigo de la Sotta and Amanda Fox—who designed the PDF version of this book and the website more elegantly than I imagined and continued to improve it with innovations and initiatives even after I was thoroughly satisfied.

The trio at Command Digital—Michael Del Gaizo, Anthony Oliveri and Robert Steffens—who made production of the paperback edition so effortless and exciting.

INTERNET LINKS

1. CHYNA'S OBITUARY:

http://www.nytimes.com/2016/04/22/arts/television/
chyna-wrestler-dead.html?_r=0

2. BOB ROSS:

http://www.todayifoundout.com/index.php/2015/09/
surprisingly-mysterious-life-artist-bob-ross/

3. BOB'S SOOTHING VOICE:

https://www.youtube.com/watch?v=ILWEXRAnQd0

4. CHICKEN SOUP FOR THE SOUL:

https://www.usatoday.com/story/money/
personalfinance/2015/05/17/jack-canfield-success-
principles/26181335/

5. JACK CANFIELD:

http://jackcanfield.com/blog/write-a-book/

6. JESSICA TATIANA LONG:

https://en.wikipedia.org/wiki/Jessica_Long

7. DIANA NYAD:

https://en.wikipedia.org/wiki/Diana_Nyad

8. BILL GROSS:

https://seekingalpha.com/article/4025832-americas-top-
unicorn-investor-idealabs-bill-gross-plots-future-in-asia

9. PEGGY GUGGENHEIM:

http://scandalouswoman.blogspot.com/2009/06/art-lover-life-of-peggy-guggenheim.html

10. SIX MILLION BUSINESSES:

https://news.gallup.com/businessjournal/180431/american-entrepreneurship-dead-alive.aspx

11. DAN CARLINSKY:

http://www.nytimes.com/1983/11/14/arts/books-famed-publicist-by-dan-carlinsky.html

12. MAMIE:

http://hidden-newyork.blogspot.com/2012/11/the-finest-house-in-new-york.html

13. JERRY SEINFELD:

https://lifehacker.com/281626/jerry-seinfelds-productivity-secret

14. DON'T BREAK THE CHAIN:

https://jamesclear.com/stop-procrastinating-seinfeld-strategy

15. KEN ROBINSON:

https://www.youtube.com/watch?v=iG9CE55wbtY

16. ENTREPRENEUR.COM:

https://www.entrepreneur.com/article/232840

17. SIX TED TALKS:

http://www.inc.com/christina-desmarais/6-ted-talks-every-entrepreneur-should-watch.html

18. WIRED VIDEO ON YOUTUBE:

https://www.youtube.com/watch?v=8_IfxPI5ObM

19. HEALTHLINE:

https://www.healthline.com/health/traumatic-events

20. CHANGING HIS DIET:

http://www.independent.co.uk/sport/tennis/revealed-the-diet-that-saved-novak-djokovic-8775333.html

21. ADDICTED TO SUGAR:

http://www.vox.com/science-and-health/2017/1/6/14167092/gary-taubes-case-against-sugar-book